This Gift of Health Provided by:

If the book you are reading is not your own and you would like to purchase a copy for yourself or a friend, simply call toll-free 800-BOOK-LOG.

Advance Praise for
The Dental Patient's Little Book of History, Humor and Trivia™

"As the author of *Billion Dollar Smile,* I know the value of a smile; and it is refreshing to see another book dedicated to the subject. My book teaches you how to OBTAIN the perfect smile; Don Dible's book MAKES you smile. Loaded with fun-filled facts, his verses will entertain you and your friends for hours."

—William Dorfman, DDS, FAACD
Author of *Billion Dollar Smile* and Founder of Discus Dental
Featured Dentist on ABC's hit "Extreme Makeover"
Frequent guest on Oprah, Larry King Live, E!, CNN and
The Tonight Show with Jay Leno

"Don Dible has produced another dental category winner with *The Dental Patient's Little Book of History, Humor and Trivia*:

This book is replete
With interesting vignettes that please the ear;
Through extensive research and use of measured verse,
He faithfully conveys stories that inform and delight readers
throughout the year."

—Arthur A. Dugoni, DDS, MS
Dean, Arthur A. Dugoni School of Dentistry
University of the Pacific, San Francisco, California

"This little book is fun on every page. However, it's hard to stop *turning* the pages. It's a *must* for the reception room."

—Peter E. Dawson, DDS
Founder and Director
Dawson Center for Advanced Dental Study

"*The Dental Patient's Little Book of History, Humor and Trivia* should be in every dental office reception area. It's fascinating, funny, and factual."

—Richard A. Glenner, DDS
Past Historian, American Academy of the History of Dentistry
Lifetime Fellow, Pierre Fauchard Academy

"This book is a fascinating, well-researched work of easy-to-read dental history facts and trivia. Dible has taken this important subject and presented it in a way that will appeal to dental teams and the entire patient community, enabling dental history to have the wider audience it richly deserves."

—Scott D. Swank, DDS
Curator, The Samuel D. Harris National Museum of Dentistry

"This is a delightful work, easy to read, and full of gems from dentistry's long history—enough to attract interest and approbation from reputable medical and dental historians. However, the primary beneficiaries of this work will be the general public and apprehensive patients awaiting care in dental offices. The intention of this author was to produce a 'light-hearted romp through dental history,' and in this he has succeeded admirably."

—Clifton O. Dummett, DDS
Distinguished Professor Emeritus and Hall of Fame Member
University of Southern California School of Dentistry
Past President, American Association of Dental Editors

"Your smile is the focus of your face, the portal to your personality. And, just as you suspected, those pearly whites have a *history*. Splashing fun facts at high speed, the verses in this volume will have you seeing your mouth in a whole new light."

—Eric K. Curtis, DDS, MAGD, ELS
Author, *Hand to Mouth: Essays on the Art of Dentistry*

"The Dental Patient's Little Book of History, Humor and Trivia makes it possible to read and learn while having fun. It also tries to take the fear out of dental care. Read! Enjoy!"

—Aletha Kowitz
Director (Retired), Bureau of Library Services
American Dental Association

"A fun and delightful read. Open it up to any page and you'll be entertained and informed!"

—James Wynbrandt
Author, *The Excruciating History of Dentistry*

"This book is a very novel approach in bringing the story of one of the most important health professions to the public. Some of the greatest advances in improving and maintaining human health were the accomplishment of dentists, and this book presents them in a lively, witty and poetic manner. Dible has covered almost every aspect of dentistry, and patients will learn just how treatment they take for granted really came about."

—Malvin E. Ring, DDS, MLS, FACD
Professor Emeritus of Dental History & Literature
State University of New York at Buffalo
Author, *Dentistry: An Illustrated History*

"He's done it again! In *The Dental Patient's Little Book of History, Humor and Trivia,* Don Dible has created a MUST-HAVE series of incredible facts and frolics every dental professional must have. Every dental professional should buy enough copies of *The Dental Patient's Little Book of History, Humor and Trivia* to share with each and every one of their patients. Dental teams and patients will laugh and learn together, all thanks to Don."

—Dr. Tom "The Gems Guy" Orent
1000 Gems Seminars & Gems Gold Dozen Coaching
www.GemsInsidersCircle.com

"The biological and mechanical art of dentistry is joyously celebrated in this happy collection of verses. The book aptly conveys the fulfillment and sense of awe we dentists regularly experience in the practice of our beloved profession."

—C.L. Brandenburg, Jr., DDS
Past President, Maryland State Dental Association
Fellow, Pierre Fauchard Academy

"*The Dental Patient's Little Book of History, Humor and Trivia* is THE book I would have written...if I had had the time! What a great concept. A year of anecdotes to share with our patients, family and friends, it deserves a place in *everyone's* office."

—Sheri B. Doniger, DDS
Editor, *Woman Dentist Journal*

"What a clever and original idea—dental historical factoids and vignettes encapsulated in the form of 366 quatrains! This light-hearted, compact tome comes complete with an excellent bibliography (including key websites) plus an index. As a result, seasoned dental historians will definitely find this work helpful in their teaching and their research. We are planning to introduce this whimsical book to our dental students and our patients."

—Arden G. Christen, DDS, MSD, MA
and Joan A. Christen, BGS, MS
Dental Historians, Indiana University School of Dentistry
Authors: *Limericks with a Smile*

Books for the Dental Profession by Don Dible

The Dental Patient's Little Book of History, Humor and Trivia™

Chicken Soup for the Dental Soul
(with Jack Canfield and Mark Victor Hansen)

Love Is the Best Medicine®
for Dental Patients and the Dental Team
(with Richard H. Madow, DDS)

The Heart of Dentistry
(with Richard H. Madow, DDS)

Kids at the Dental Office
(with Richard H. Madow, DDS)

It's All about Smiles
(with Richard H. Madow, DDS)

We Care!
(with Richard H. Madow, DDS)

All books are available through the distributor, DMD House, at www.dmdhousebooks.com. Select titles are also available through major dental supply houses.

The Dental Patient's Little Book of History, Humor and Trivia™

A Lighthearted Romp through Dental History
—Set in 366 Daily Rhymes—
Designed to Delight and Inform
Dental Teams and Patients Everywhere

Don Dible

Illustrated by Richard Golueke

A

Series Book

Murrieta, California

THE DENTAL PATIENT'S LITTLE BOOK OF HISTORY, HUMOR AND TRIVIA
A LIGHTHEARTED ROMP THROUGH DENTAL HISTORY
—SET IN 366 DAILY RHYMES—
DESIGNED TO DELIGHT AND INFORM DENTAL TEAMS AND PATIENTS EVERYWHERE

published by DMD HOUSE

International Standard Book Number: 978-0-9713148-7-0
Library of Congress Control Number: 2005910442

DMD HOUSE logo and LOVE IS THE BEST MEDICINE®
series title logo created by
Cha Designs, Redwood City, California 650.365.9446.

Heart and Rx logo designed by
American Business Card, Scottsdale, Arizona 800.555.2234.

Little Book of History, Humor and Trivia logo
designed by David Anderson

Cover design and verse illustrations created by
Richard Golueke, Hercules, California 510.964.0805

Printed in the United States of America.

Fourth Printing

For information, contact:
DMD HOUSE
29925 Rose Blossom Drive, Suite 300
Murrieta, CA 92563-4735

In Memoriam

To the late Rudigear Neumarker, DDS,
Beloved dentist to the Dible family,
This book of verse is dedicated;
As we strive to honor his memory.

Dr. Rudi faithfully served the three of us
For more than 30 years;
His early death from pancreatic cancer
Brought everyone to tears.

During the height of the Cold War,
Teenage Rudi escaped the Communist regime.
After leaving the repression of East Germany,
Life in America fulfilled his greatest dream.

Rudi's office was located in Palo Alto
On the campus of Stanford University.
But today he conducts his practice
In a realm that's much more heavenly.

CONTENTS

Please Read This First xvii

The Toothworm xx

January

- HesiRe, the world's first dentist-of-record
- What the Tooth Fairy does with all those teeth
- 4,000+ year-old acupuncture remedy for toothache pain
- Pierre Fauchard,
  The *French* Father of Modern Dentistry
- Dr. Joseph Lister, antiseptic pioneer after whom Listerine is named
- Talk show host Rosie O'Donnell weighs in for Listerine
- Plus humor and trivia! 2

February

- Aluminum dentures
- Apollonia, Patron Saint of Dentistry
- Greene Vardiman Black,
  The *American* Father of Modern Dentistry
- Early, non-electric tooth drills
- Plus humor and trivia! 18

March

- The official color of dentistry
- Early toothbrushes
- Discovery of X-rays
- First recorded extractions
- Halitosis facts
- The Mummy's teeth
- Paul Revere, patriot and dentist
- George Washington's dentures
- Plus humor and trivia! 34

April

- The National Museum of Dentistry
- Tuscany, home of the world's first dentures
- First American-authored dental book
- Bishop Aylmer's toothy sacrifice for Queen Elizabeth I
- Dr. John Harvey Kellogg, the corn flake king
- Nitrous oxide
- Ether
- Cocaine
- Novocain
- The flamboyant, filthy-rich, Dr. Painless Parker
- Plus humor and trivia! 48

May

- America's first woman dentist
- Introduction of mass-marketed toothbrushes
- Author Jack London's South Seas dentistry
- Clinical names for each of your teeth
- Clinical names for the surfaces of your teeth
- Amusing Vermont denture law and women's rights
- Plaque, calculus, gallstones, and kidney stones, a fascinating—but unhealthy—quartet
- Edward Hartley Angle, Father of Orthodontics
- Plus humor and trivia! 62

June

- Actor James Dean's dentures
- Amazing earliest fillings
- First enameled gold crowns
- Childbirth and maternal dental health
- Dr. Bernard J. Cigrand, dentist and Father of Flag Day
- Evolution of the dental chair
- "Doc" Holliday, the gunslinging dentist
- "Jeopardy" training
- Plus humor and trivia! 76

July

- The oddly coincidental, same-day deaths of former-presidents Thomas Jefferson and John Adams
- Alfred Moss and Jack Miller, Indy 500 dentists
- The Baltimore College of Dental Surgery, world's first dental school
- Peculiar dental standards for Civil War military service
- Dr. C. Edmund Kells, Jr., dental X-ray pioneer
- Differences between dog and cat teeth
- Robert Tanner Freeman, world's first African American dental school graduate
- World's first dental school graduate
- What side do you chew your food on?
- Troop oral health lessons of WWI, military-directed personal hygiene programs in WWII, and the impact on the post-war civilian population
- Plus humor and trivia! 92

August

- Ancient history's first dental hygienists
- Willoughby Dayton Miller, American discoverer of the microbial cause of tooth decay
- Tooth harvesting from dead soldiers after Napoleon's defeat at Waterloo
- Strange ingredients in toothpaste through the ages
- First mass-merchandising of toothpaste in collapsible metal tubes
- Juliette A. Southard, world's first dental assistant and founding president of the American Dental Assistants Association
- Irene Newman, America's first dental hygienist
- Dr. Alfred Fones, founder of the world's first school for dental hygienists
- Plus humor and trivia! 106

September

- Marco Polo, Parisian dentist Nicolas Dubois de Chémant, and the invention of porcelain dentures
- Introduction of hypnosis as a dental anesthetic
- Swedish orthopedic surgeon Per-Ingvar Brånemark, the discovery of osseointegration, and the invention of dental implants
- Plus humor and trivia! 122

October

- Understanding periodontitis and bone loss
- Lucy Beaman Hobbs, the world's first woman dental school graduate
- Charles Goodyear, inventor of vulcanized rubber
- The Goodyear Vulcanite denture saga—from monopoly to *murder*
- Plus humor and trivia 138

November

- Dr. Jonathan Taft, mentor to Lucy Beaman Hobbs, the world's first *woman* dental school graduate, and sponsor of Lucy Gray, the world's first *African American woman* dental school graduate
- Bruxism (one-in-three people brux): What it is and what to do about it
- Ophthalmic surgeon Charles D. Kelman, MD, and how a visit to the *dentist* sparked an idea for outpatient cataract treatment that has helped more than 100 million patients
- Dr. William S. Halsted and the romantic history of surgical gloves
- Bill Baker, oral and maxillofacial surgeon and U.S. Hockey Team Defenseman in the 1980 Winter Olympiad where the U.S. seriously stomped some Russian butt
- Plus humor and trivia! 154

December

- Toothpick manufacturing in the U.S. and Japan
- Thomas Wiltberger Evans, an American dental school graduate who went to Paris, was named Surgeon-Dentist to the imperial court of Napoleon III, Emperor of France, served as ambassador-without-portfolio for France in meetings with Lincoln, Seward, and Grant on the eve of the American Civil War, made millions in Paris real estate, and rescued the Spanish-born Empress of France from the guillotine
- The founding of the Hispanic Dental Association
- The founding of the [African American] National Dental Association
- The founding of the American Dental Association
- Plus humor and trivia! 168

Acknowledgments 185

Selected Bibliography 187

Index 197

ADA Foundation 205

PLEASE READ THIS FIRST!

My favorite air carrier is Southwest Airlines. I really enjoy the inventiveness of some of the preflight announcements. While serving the safety needs of passengers, the cabin attendants also help establish an atmosphere of camaraderie among planeloads of strangers. Here are a couple of examples:

"There may be 50 ways to leave your lover, but there are only *four* ways out of this airplane."

"Welcome aboard Southwest Flight 1234 with service to XYZ. To operate your seatbelt, insert the metal tab into the buckle and pull tight. It works just like every other seatbelt; and if you don't know how to operate one, you probably shouldn't be out in public unsupervised. In the event of a sudden loss of cabin pressure, oxygen masks will descend from the ceiling. Stop screaming, grab the mask, and pull it over your face. If you have a small child traveling with you, secure your mask before assisting with theirs. If you are traveling with two small children, decide *now* which one you love more."

Just as flight crews thank passengers for flying their airline, my wife and I would like to thank you for your purchase of this book—the royalties will come in handy when we pay our mortgage and add to our retirement fund. (As with my other paperback dental books, a portion of the revenue from the sale of *this* book will be donated to the ADA Foundation.) I'd also like to tell you about the journey in the pages ahead and my qualifications for accompanying you.

First, I'm not a dentist, and that isn't a bad thing. I bring the perspective of an informed patient to this endeavor. (I've been a model dental patient for 70 years and have produced seven dental books since 1999!) While researching this project, hardly an hour went by without my discovering some exciting, delightful, "*gee whiz*, my readers are gonna love this" tidbit of information. I continually interrupted my long-suffering wife of

38 years to share some intriguing new fact I'd discovered. I also found myself thinking, "I'll bet most *dentists* don't know *that* bit of history, and dental patients will be amused-delighted-intrigued if I share it with them!"

Now don't get the wrong idea about my dental expertise; as will be explained in the Acknowledgments section of this book, I've been successful in recruiting numerous dentists to review this material in a heartfelt effort to ensure that no health-related information *whatsoever* is less than one-hundred percent accurate!

Second, I'm not a historian. *The Dentist's Little Book of History, Humor and Trivia* is not intended to be a work of dry scholarship loaded with footnotes you need a magnifying glass to read. Before I began this manuscript, I was well aware of how barbaric the early days of medicine were. As I pursued my research, I discovered that early dentistry was not exempt from the ignorance, superstition, "magic," religious interference, and quackery that characterized early medicine.

Again, with an eye to accuracy, I have benefitted enormously from the pre-publication input of a number of recognized dental historians.

What I've found *awesome* is how far dentistry has come in the last couple of hundred years. Patients no longer suffer from "toothworms" and "the humors." They no longer have dead mice placed at the site of a toothache to relieve pain. Better yet, they are not instructed to *eat* dead mice to relieve pain!

The emergence of outstanding dental schools, hundreds of regular technical meetings, hundreds of professional journals, and state licensing now ensure uniformly high standards of practice by dental professionals. Patient education, the availability of all manner of products to serve the cause of daily oral hygiene, and fluoridation of our water have all produced remarkable reductions in tooth loss. A variety of technologies have emerged that make for impressive dental diagnostics as well as patient comfort. Furthermore, remarkable progress has been made in the field of cosmetic dentistry. Patients' teeth now look better than they have at any time in human history!

One more thing about the treatment of history in this book: From time to time in researching the text, calender dates (day and month) of special note popped up. (What would history be without *dates*?) It made logical sense to tie these citations to the corresponding day and month headings around which the book is formatted—regardless of the year (or century) being studied. So don't expect a linear, Garden-of-Eden-to-the-Present narrative. Sequentially, the presentation jumps around...*a lot!*

Third, I'm not a poet; while my quatrains may rhyme (mostly, sort of), the preponderance of them are dreadfully lacking in *meter* (a uniform number of syllables in each line—I just looked it up). My objective here is to amuse and inform. I'll let you be the judge of my poetic prowess. However, I *have* written more than 50 books in the last 35-plus years, so I'm very comfortable as a wordsmith.

I was recently privileged to assist a longtime client in formatting a book of quatrains. As soon as that project was finished, I began researching this history of dentistry. Almost immediately, it occurred to me that framing these dental facts and humor in quatrain format might make for lighter, easier reading. As you make your way through the following 366 quatrains—one for each day of the year (including Leap Day), I hope you agree.

Finally, if you are a dentist and enjoy this book, please consider purchasing copies to give to your patients. You might even consider recommending me as a speaker at your next dental conference. If you are a patient, please tell your friends how much you enjoyed reading this book and suggest they get copies for themselves. And last-but-not-least, thank you for joining me on this flight of discovery through dental history. I hope you enjoy reading it half as as much as I enjoyed researching and writing it.

Don Dible
Murrieta, California

THE TOOTHWORM

The toothworm is the earliest recorded explanation of the cause of toothache. A cure may be found in the following inscription on a tablet from Nineveh, former capital of the Assyrian Empire located on the Tigris River opposite what is now Mosul, Iraq. The tablet may be found today in the British Museum.

THE LEGEND OF THE TOOTHWORM

After Anu had created the heavens,
The heavens created the earth,
The earth created the rivers,
The rivers created the brooks,
The brooks created the swamps,
The swamps created the worm,
Then came the worm before Shamash [the Sun God]
Before Ea [the God of the Deep] came her tears:
"What willst thou give me to eat and destroy?"
"Ripe figs will I give thee."
"What good are ripe figs to me? Take me up and let me reside between the teeth and the gums, so that I may destroy the blood of the tooth and ruin their strength; the roots of the tooth I will eat."
"Since thou hast said this, Worm,
May Ea strike thee with the power of her fist."

This is the magic ritual:
Mix together beer, the sa-kil-bir plant, and oil.
Then repeat the magic formula thrice and place the mixture on the tooth.

The tablet from which this text was taken is apparently a copy of an older record. The concept of worms causing dental decay was accepted without question for centuries in Western Civilization. The notion was not formally rejected until 1728 by Pierre Fauchard, the French father of modern dentistry discussed at length in the January quatrains.

The Dental Patient's

Little Book of History, Humor and Trivia™

A Lighthearted Romp through Dental History
—Set in 366 Daily Rhymes—
Designed to Delight and Inform
Dental Teams and Patients Everywhere

JANUARY

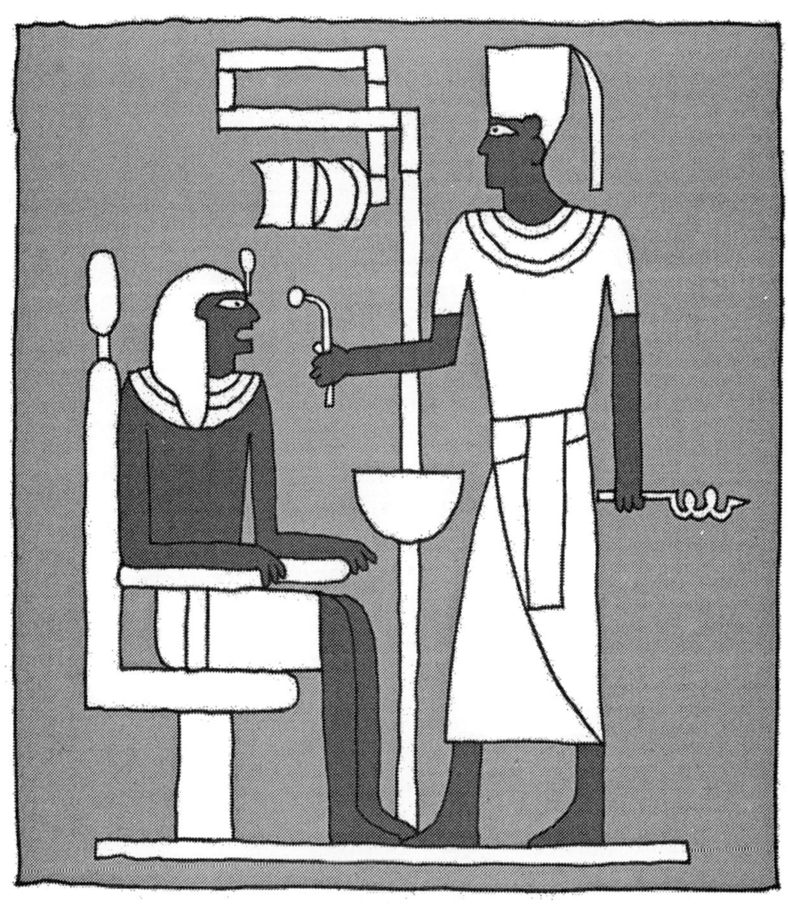

January 1

TOOTH DOC TO THE PHARAOHS

The earliest dentist of whom we have record is HesiRe.

He lived in the Old Kingdom,
3rd Dynasty (2650-2575 BC), give or take.

Polished wood panels on display in
Cairo's Egyptian Museum feature hieroglyphs

According him the title "Chief Toothist" and portray,
in splendid robes, this *First Master of the Toothache.*

January 2

THANK THE GREEKS!

Odont is Greek for "tooth."

When the early Romans conquered Greece, they learned about teeth from captured Greek teachers and then gave tooth their own moniker—in Latin, of course: *dent.*

It was the Old French, next-door Mediterranean neighbors to the Italians with whom they shared gossip and health information, who awarded the appellation *dentiste* to those who worked on teeth.

And, in the 1750s, it was the British—across the English Channel—who adapted the word from French dental pioneers and *dentist* appeared in print with an English accent.

January 3

RITE OF PASSAGE

Through the millennia and across the ages,
The loss of a child's first teeth
Has called for a *ritual* that, to future generations,
Loving parents desired to bequeath.

January 4

SANTA CLAUS, THE EASTER BUNNY, AND *WHO?*

1927 marked a North American "first";
That's when Ester Watkins Arnold wrote a three-act playlet
In which "The Tooth Fairy"
got an official name AND the title role!
The rest is "modern history"
that no living mom or dad is likely to forget.

January 5

THE $64,000 ANSWER!

"What happens to all those teeth?"

Here's an answer every child wants but rarely gets:

"The Tooth Fairy whisks them off to Fairyland where

They're magically transformed into Dogtoothed Violets."

[N.B. The eight-page script for Arnold's playlet was originally circulated by the Eldridge Entertainment House of Franklin, Ohio and Denver, Colorado for 25 cents a copy. We can thank the late Dr. Rosemary Wells, founder of the now-defunct Tooth Fairy Museum, for this bit of trivia.]

January 6

GREEN AND YELLOW CAT

The English first called the plant "Lion's Tooth"

Because, like a lion's teeth, its leaf edge is indented;

But the French prevailed with *dent de lion*—teeth of the lion.

No matter what *you* call them, dandelions
can make your weed-hating gardener demented.

January 7

FOOT-IN-MOUTH CURE!

Historians tell us that the Chinese were using acupuncture to ease toothache pain as far back as 2700 BC!

For this malady, the needle insertion point is located (don't laugh) on the *Kidney* Meridian, one of 14 main meridians identified long ago in an ancient time zone.

But it gets weirder!

The actual insertion point for toothache, called *Taixi*, is just behind the inner *ankle bone*!

January 8

PIERRE FAUCHARD

The "Father of Modern Dentistry,"
claim the French,

Was Pierre Fauchard, born in 1678.

At the ripe old age of fifty, he published
Le chirurgien dentiste [*The Surgeon Dentist*],

A two-volume, 863-page text hailed as *great*!

January 9

WHAT WAS THE BIG DEAL?

Why did Fauchard's book enjoy so much fame?

Advances in European dentistry at the time

Were treated as deep, dark, professional "secrets,"
rarely revealed to one's "competitive" peers.

Fauchard skillfully gathered the *best* of the existing practices
and published them in a manner both scientific and sublime!

January 10

RESTORATION

Fauchard's volumes were considered a wonder;

He explained dental anatomy and tooth anomalies.

He even described how to
replant knocked-out teeth—

A true blessing for roughhousing families.

Pierre Fauchard (1678-1761)

January 11

PF Was a PR Maven

The fact is, textbooks on oral health
Date back to the ancient Greeks.
It was big printings on Gutenberg presses
That helped give Fauchard the fame he did seek.

January 12

SUPINE

Fauchard pioneered the cause of patient dignity;
His book recommends
a comfortable armchair…Heaven-sent.
"No longer," he proclaimed,
"should the patient lie on the floor
And grasp the dentist's leg
while undergoing treatment."

January 13

ROYAL PULL

Fauchard's clients were the royalty of France;
Political connections he regularly did build.
With deft skill, he engineered the independence
Of the first French Dental Guild.

January 14

HIGHER STANDARDS

Once the dental guild was established,
Fauchard and others codified standards of practice;
This soon drove fakers and charlatans
From the bridges and street corners of Paris.

January 15

ORAL EXAM

If you wanted to join the French Dental Guild,
You were required to pass an entrance test.
Thorough knowledge of Fauchard's *The Surgeon Dentist*
Guaranteed your scoring with the best.

January 16

FOREVERMORE

Fauchard's contributions to dentistry
are not likely to be forgotten;

The international Pierre Fauchard Academy
continues to perpetuate his name.

PFA is an honorary organization that supports
the highest ideals of dentistry worldwide.

Membership in PFA confers upon each inductee
a much-coveted measure of recognition and fame.

January 17

HIS GREATEST ACCOMPLISHMENT

Although *The Surgeon Dentist*
contributed greatly to the world's oral health

(Many of Fauchard's ideas
are current today, without question)

His most valuable gift to society

Was establishing dentistry as a *profession!*

January 18

PARSON'S, ANYONE?

Ammonia's been a household cleaning fluid for centuries;

It's also a strong antimicrobial.

Ammonia is a major component of urine,

The Surgeon Dentist recommends urine as a mouthwash;
tho' most users decline to provide a testimonial.

January 19

WHEN IN ROME

The earliest *documented* use of urine-as-mouthwash
Occurred among the ancient Greeks,
who considered the results most benificent.
The first-urine-of-the-day was thought to be the strongest,
But Romans of the time considered pee from
Spain and *Portugal* to be *absolutely* the most potent!

January 20

VANITY OBLIGED

The menu of services offered by 17th-century
London barber-surgeons was extensive:

Teeth cleaning, tooth extraction, bloodletting, cupping,
boil lancing, a haircut, or, of course, a shave.

For the first procedure, toothpicks and
linen scraps were usually employed.

After plaque-scraping, an *aqua fortis* rinse produced the
fashionably white finish *everyone* who was *anyone* did crave.

January 21

FROM THE LATIN

Aqua, water + *fortis*, strong = strong water.

Yes, *aqua fortis* IS strong water;
NITRIC ACID is its *other* name!

Applied to teeth improperly diluted
and without the greatest of care,

That stuff removed *all* the enamel, and in no time flat,
these barber-surgeon victims were permanently
out of "The Dating Game"!

January 22

CUISINE CANIBALIS

To a large extent, human history
is a never-ending tale of war.

Until modern times, battle wounds were synonymous
with amputation and/or gangrene.

French microbiologist and chemist Louis Pasteur
(yes, the *pasteur*ized milk guy) was the first
to suggest that chemical solutions could
be used to thwart this *sepsis* menace.

Thus began the process of removing human flesh
from the menu of microorganism cuisine.

January 23

AUTHOR, AUTHOR

Enter Joseph Lister, a British surgeon
who took his continuing education seriously.

He read Pasteur's paper,
tested carbolic acid (phenol) on many a wound,

Discovered that it markedly reduced
the incidence of gangrene,

And, in the March 16, 1867, edition of *The Lancet,*
published what he found.

January 24

SQUEAKY CLEAN

Lister's landmark paper,
"Antiseptic Principle of the Practice of Surgery,"

Was an immediate—though to some, controversial—professional *sensation*.

This gave Lister the platform from which to urge his colleagues to wear clean gloves and wash their hands with a 5% carbolic acid solution before operations.

He also urged that surgical instruments be *sterilized* before use—at the time, a troublesome innovation!

January 25

FAME

In 1869, Lister became Professor of Surgery at Edinburgh University.

By then, his lectures attracted audiences of 400 colleagues or more, plus many a student.

Considered "The Father of Modern Surgery," Lister's principal contribution was sterility and extreme cleanliness in all medical procedures.

In 1883, King Edward VII of England made him *Baron* Lister of Lyme Regis; but the thing that made his name a household word was a *mouthwash* he didn't even invent!

January 26

Disinfectant

120 years ago, the original amber-colored Listerine antiseptic was formulated by Dr. Joseph Lawrence and Jordan Wheat Lambert.

The product was named in honor of Sir Joseph Lister, their esteemed contemporary.

In 1884, the Lambert Company was formed to manufacture and market Listerine to the medical community.

The potion was soon recognized by the *dental* profession as an excellent antiseptic for oral surgery.

January 27

Better Than No Breath at All

By 1914, the effectiveness and popularity of the Listerine formula made it

One of the first *prescription* items ever to become available *over-the-counter*—a fantastic marketing win!

Thus was established the *mouthwash* category of oral care consumer products.

To differentiate itself from the quick-to-emerge competition, Listerine positioned its product as the enemy of "halitosis"—*unpleasant breath* in Latin.

January 28

PRIZE-WINNING MARKETING

After the *halitosis* campaign, Listerine continued its history-making promotions with slogans like:

"Always a bridesmaid, never a bride,"

"The taste you hate twice a day," and "It's dynamite against germs."

Today, Listerine is number one in market share; there appears to be no place for the competition to hide!

January 29

BIG MISTAKE

In the mid-1990s, a Listerine competitor named talk-show host Rosie O'Donnell the least-kissable celebrity in the U.S.

Understandably irked, O'Donnell teamed up with Listerine to give $1,000 to the For All Kids Foundation every time she kissed a guest on the air.

This provided positive publicity for Listerine and harsh publicity for the competitor.

There's gotta be a lesson in here somewhere!

[N.B. O'Donnell raised more than $500,000 for her children's charity during the run of this program.]

January 30

I CAN SEE CLEARLY NOW!

Called eyeteeth, cuspids, dogteeth, canines, or fangs,

They're the four pointed conical teeth located between the premolars and the incisors.

The upper eyeteeth are situated just under the eyes.

In the early 2nd Century AD, the Greek physician Galen wrongly hypothesized that the nerves which supply the upper cuspids are connected to the eyes. Knowing that, don't you feel wiserz?

[N.B. Most of the medical views of Claudius Galen (c. 129-c. 216 AD) were on the mark. In his lifetime, he became the most famous physician in the Roman Empire.]

January 31

SPOONERISM

Ever say, "Wave the sails" when what you meant was "Save the whales?"

In the 19th Century, Oxford University's Rev. William Archibald Spooner regularly mouthed these verbal discombobulations—even when praying.

Before long, his name became synonymous with the problem.

Apparently, whenever Spooner's tongue got caught in his eyeteeth, it became impossible for him to see what he was saying.

FEBRUARY

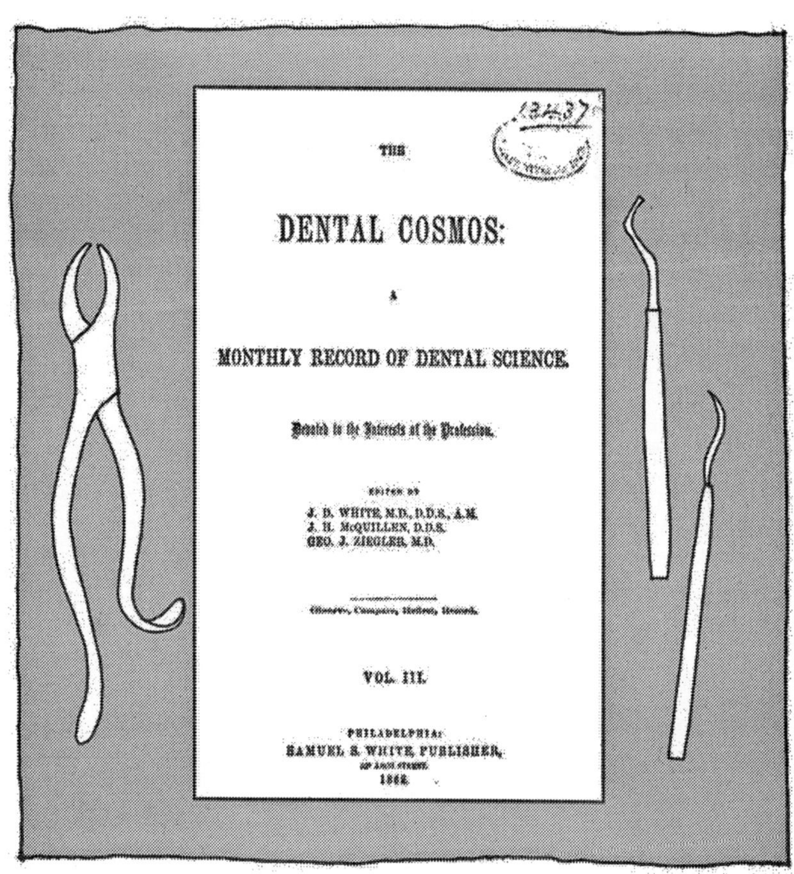

February 1

DENTAL COSMOS

The first *enduring* national journal for American dentistry was *Dental Cosmos, a Monthly Record of Dental Science.*

Introduced in 1847 as a newsletter by Jones & White, (Later the S.S. White Dental Manufacturing Company), *Dental Cosmos* became a *journal* in 1859.

On the illustrious history of early American dentistry, this proprietary publication still shines a brilliant light.

February 2

MERGERS AND PHILANTHROPY

In 1936, *Dental Cosmos* merged with the *Journal of the American Dental Association, JADA.*

Decades later at the University of Michigan—with funding from Colgate—

Dental Cosmos was converted to electronic format

So history buffs with Internet access can read this stuff *anytime*—early in the day or late!

February 3

CONFEDERATE DENTURES

"Aluminum, *par excellence,* is *the* metal most perfectly adapted as a base for artificial teeth...."

So said former Confederate dental surgeon Dr. James Baxter Bean in Volume VIII of the 1867 issue of the aforementioned *Dental Cosmos* journal.

He continues, "...the whole piece can be kept more cleanly and sweeter in the mouth than vulcanite ever can be...; plates worn in the mouth for weeks without cleaning present no change whatsoever."

It was 50 years later, though, before the aluminum denture was re-introduced, once again, by way of the military arsenal!

[N.B. Vulcanite, a hard-rubber compound, was colored dark red when manufactured for denture use.]

February 4

THE "AMEX" DENTURE OF WWI

In 1917, the U.S. Army decided to reopen Bean's investigation upon determining that the then-popular Vulcanite dentures weren't rugged enough for wartime use.

As the Confederate dental surgeon had pointed out, aluminum dentures were stronger, lighter, and cheaper than Vulcanite.

They also had greater durability and ease of repair.

Oddly, nobody commented on the "metal-mouth" appearance of the Army-christened "Amex," an esthetic factor certain to inspire enemy fright!

February 5

WAR IS HELL!

In June 1917, two American dentists—both lieutenants—successfully conducted research on casting aluminum dentures at an Allied facility in France.

The makeshift "casting flask" used for the mold was part of a "Soixante Quinze" (75mm) shell.

The rest of the hardware was also constructed using materials at hand; and on November 7, 1918, the Allied Expeditionary Forces dental labs were ordered to begin large-scale fabrication of the denture.

However, the armistice—announced just four days later—brought that barbaric war *and* the aluminum denture project to a halt. All's well that ends well!

February 6

BIBLICAL COMMENTARY

Factoid: Teeth are mentioned 42 times in the Bible; here are just two examples.

Exodus 21:27: "And if he [the slave owner] smite out his manservant's tooth, or his maidservant's tooth, he shall let him [the servant] go free for his tooth's sake."

The Book of Daniel makes reference to a night-vision [night*mare*?] "fourth beast" with *iron* teeth!

Wow; and you thought *aluminum* teeth were scary; *iron* choppers are enough to make *anyone* shiver and quake!

February 7

CIRCA 200 AD

In pagan Rome, a painful punishment
much less severe than crucifixion

Was routinely meted out: tooth extraction.

Deaconess Apollonia of Alexandria, an aged, Christian
virgin noted for self-sacrifice and charitable deeds,

Was marked for torture
(tooth extraction after her jaws were smashed)
by Emperor Philip during festivities commemorating
the millenary of the Roman Empire unless she
recanted her faith and gave their idols adoration.

February 8

THE MAKING OF A MARTYR

Not only were all of Apollonia's teeth ripped out;

When this righteously-defiant woman continued to deny the Roman idols,

She was threatened with death by fire.

Rather than renounce her beliefs, Apollonia ran into the waiting flames—an act deemed, by some, suicidal.

[N.B. Apollonia died violently for her faith, hence she is known in the Catholic Church as a "red" martyr. A "white" martyr is one whose life is a total offering to God, a "dying" to the world and its allurements.]

February 9

CELEBRATION

On the calendar of the Roman Catholic Church,

St. Apollonia is the patron saint of dentists and toothache sufferers, canonized in 249 AD.

The official date for remembering her heroic acts is February 9.

For more than a millennium, millions have asked her intercession to relieve toothache pain with a prayerful plea.

February 10

LOOK MA, NO CAVITIES!

In the U.S., February is
National Children's Dental Health Month.

Teaching kids proper oral hygiene skills

Is the responsibility of every loving parent.
(♥ your children; ♥ their teeth!)

Consider this: There is no more cost-effective way to spare kids toothaches *and* lower future dental bills.

February 11

FIRST AID

If you completely knock out a permanent tooth,
first pick it up by the TOP, not the roots.

If you can, place it back into
the socket from which it came.

If you can't replant the tooth, store it
in milk or protect it with plastic wrap.

Minutes count; see your dentist ASAP
or the tooth will die...that'd be a shame!

February 12

SMILE PROTECTORS

If you participate in contact sports,

And want to avoid tooth loss from collision,

You'll surely want to have a dentist make
you your very own *mouthguard*,

Like the ones NFL players wear on television.

February 13

GREENE VARDIMAN BLACK, MD, DDS, ScD, LLD

The "Father of Modern Dentistry," Americans claim,

Was born in 1836 to an Illinois cabinet-maker/farmer
and christened Greene Vardiman Black.

"G.V." is best known for his hundreds
of groundbreaking papers and books

As well as innovations in methodology
and instrumentation...Black was no *hack*!

February 14

SELF-SCHOOLED

One of five offspring, there were two things
young Black disliked intensely:

School classrooms (three months each winter)
and the chores of a farm.

A plaque erected in his honor
at Northwestern University states:

"He roamed the woods with dog, [fishing] rod and gun,
and became intimately acquainted with every tree,
animal and insect...." This lad had folkloric charm!

February 15

NATURAL STUDENT

That same Northwestern plaque continues:

"He thus developed in nature's laboratory

Methods of clear thinking and logical deduction."

Now we begin to see Black's potential
for making *American dental history*.

February 16

THE INTERN

Starting at age seventeen, G.V. learned medicine
Under the tutelage of Dr. Thomas Black, his older brother.
Four years later, G.V. concluded that
the financial rewards of *another* profession, *dentistry*,
Would enable him to court and marry a "significant other."

February 17

BRIEF APPRENTICESHIP

At age 21, G.V. commenced on-the-job dental training
Under the highly-respected Dr. J.C. Spears.
A quick-study, G.V. opened his own practice
After apprenticing for only one yearzz!

February 18

MILITARY SERVICE

Not long afterward, though,
the American Civil War began.

In 1862, G.V. patriotically enlisted
in the 129th Illinois Volunteers.

Soon after, on a scouting mission, he tore his knee on a rusty,
barbed-wire fence; the wound became infected; and he was
hospitalized for six months, narrowly avoiding leg amputation.

Not until his discharge was Black able to
pursue an uninterrupted dental career.

February 19

TEACHING: THE BEST WAY TO LEARN!

It was in his Jacksonville, Illinois, office
that G.V. first became famous;

There, he set new standards of quality and
craftsmanship in restorations and fillings.

He also maintained an extensive machine
shop and chemistry lab on the premises.

While Black's experiments and his care for patients were
engaging, it was *teaching* that he found most fulfilling!

February 20

DENTAL MECCA

Before long, G.V.'s office was receiving a steady
stream of uninvited-but-welcome visitors—

Other dentists eager to learn from him.

What amazed one and all was
Black's eagerness—his *passion*—

For filling their enlightenment-seeking cups to the brim!

GREENE VARDIMAN BLACK (1836-1915)

February 21

LAST WORDS

In 1897, Black became Chair of Operative Dentistry at the Northwestern University Dental School and, later, its Dean.

To his Jackson practice, he said a fond "Goodbye."

A lifelong lover of nature, the last words G.V. was heard to utter before meeting his Maker were:

"Trees...Flowers...Sky."

February 22

LEGACY

Among G.V.'s oeuvre are included:

Formations of Poisons by Microörganisms (1884)
[Agatha Christie fans, take note!]

Dental Anatomy (1891), and the four-volume
Operative Dentistry (1908).

Even today's dentists will find useful stuff
in the Black Books this venerable doctor wrote!

[N.B. Another G.V. Black contribution to his
profession was coinage of the term, "dental plaque."]

February 23

AMALGAM

Those silver-colored fillings
in most people's teeth are made of amalgam.

After dentists drilled the decay out of
cavities, the excavation required a fix.

For 100-plus years, they have filled the holes
with Dr. Black's amalgam alloy formula:

67% silver, 27% tin, 5% copper, 1% zinc,
And a bit of mercury to moisten the mix.

[N.B. You may be interested to know that the most
common source of silver used in the amalgams
of Black's day was filings from U.S. coins.]

February 24

METALLURGY LESSON

"So what's the big deal with amalgam?"
you may ask; we'll tell you without hesitation.

Some early fillings shrank after placement,
rattled around for a while, and then fell out.

Others expanded and split the poor patient's tooth.

Clearly, Black's *stable* amalgam was the solution,
of that history shows there's no doubt!

February 25

COMPOSITES

Widely introduced in the 1960s
and continually being improved,

Bonded dental composites are the latest filling innovation.

A tooth-colored plastic mixture, they are esthetically
pleasing but require more time to place than amalgam

So they cost more, but give
appearance-conscious patients a sense of elation.

[N.B. Michael Buonocore invented composite
(tooth-colored) fillings at the Rochester, New York,
Eastman Dental Center in 1955.]

February 26

SMALL EXCAVATIONS

The first step in saving a tooth
Is purging the cavity of diseased tissue.
Anthropologists tell us that early "dentists"
Made use of picks and small scissors
to deal with this issue.

February 27

THE FINGER DRILL

As the importance of caries removal was better understood,
A *new* gizmo appeared on the scene:
a small metal rod tipped with a double-edged cutter.
The spindle was twirled twixt the thumb and
forefinger while the dull end rested against
the dentist's palm to apply pressure.
"This is a painfully slow process,"
patients were often heard to mutter.

[N.B. The back end of the drill was covered
with a metal thimble to prevent the
dentist from drilling a hole in his palm.]

February 28

THE BOW DRILL

Millennia ago, Man hunted with bows and arrows;
He also used a "Boy Scout style"
stick and bow to kindle a blaze.
Using essentially the same "technology,"
Man made holes in beads with a small "bow drill"?
Removing caries with a "jeweler's" bow drill
was simply dental evolution's next phase!

February 29

SPEED FREAK

In 1871, dentist James B. Morrison patented
The first commercially manufactured
foot-treadle dental engine—
at the time, *state-of-the-art* mechanical artistry.
This inexpensive, mechanized tool supplied
dental burs with enough speed
(2,000 rpm—20 times faster than hand-powered drills)
To cut enamel and dentin smoothly
and quickly, *revolutionizing* (no pun intended)
the practice of dentistry.

MARCH

March 1

SPANNING THE GAP

Need to replace a missing tooth?
Consider the attractive Maryland Bridge.
It's a wire-free cosmetic solution
Bonded to its neighbors by adhesive—just a smidge.

March 2

ELIZABETHAN "MISTER MANNERS"

"Pick not they teeth with they knyfe
Nor with they fyngers ende,
But take a stick, or some cleane thyng,
Then doe you not offende."

[N.B. Excerpted from the *Boke of Nurture*
by Hugh Rhodes, 1577.]

March 3

SHOCKING DISCOVERY!

In 1875, George F. Green patented the first electric drill
While employed at the S.S. White Company
as a mechanic.

Since most American dental offices
were not yet electrified at the time,

His invention was considered by some premature...
by others, *Satanic!*

March 4

EAT DIRT!

"...His fellow warriors, many a one,

Fall 'round him to the earth and *bite the dust.*"

Who can we thank for this colorful phrase?

Homer, in his two-thousand-plus year-old *Iliad*;
to him, give recognition we must.

[N.B. The Greek-English translation above is credited
to the American poet, William Cullen Bryant, in 1870.]

March 5

THE COLOR PURPLE

Each profession has its official color,
All-important when lining academic gowns.
For dentistry, the hue is *lilac*,
not lavender or purple as many folks think.
With *that* settled; now let's seat those crowns!

[N.B. The color lilac was selected by the
National Association of Dental Faculties in 1897.]

March 6

EARLY TOOTHBRUSHES

The first "toothbrushes" on record, called "siwaks,"
were found in ancient Egyptian tombs.
Made of twigs and thin branches,
the ends were frayed into soft fibers of wood.
Sean Connery can be seen "brushing" his teeth
with one of these "instruments"
In "Robin and Marian,"
the 1976 movie in which he starred as Robin Hood.

[N.B. Today, in many Third-World countries,
the siwak or "chew stick" is still in wide use.]

March 7

TOMB RAIDER

At about the same time in history—
Exploration of Egyptian tombs does reveal—
An unusual *horseshoe*-shaped instrument was employed
For scraping the tongue, no doubt,
and enhancing breath appeal!

March 8

OF DUTCH EXTRACTION

Little Billy was full of mischief;
That he lacked manners,
his geography classmates had no doubt.
When Sally wouldn't share some of her candies,
He told others, "I hope they Rotterdam teeth out."

March 9

FATHER OF THE X-RAY

Wilhelm Conrad Röntgen, a professor of physics and director of the physics institute at the University of Wurzburg in Bavaria,
Discovered X-rays in 1895.
For that, he won the first Nobel Prize in Physics in 1901,
And his contribution to dentistry
("Open wide, and then bite down on the bitewings, please.")
will forever survive.

[N.B.1. Eugene Solomon Talbot, MD (1847-1924), Professor of Dental Surgery at the Northwestern Woman's Medical School, was the first person to use X-rays for orthodontic diagnosis.]

[N.B.2. Dr. Howard Riley Raper introduced bitewings in a 1925 *Journal of the American Dental Association* article.]

March 10

SMALL FRY

Pits and fissures abound
In the teeth of 'most every young child.
Sealants, like a coat of paint, can plug these holes
And stop cavities from driving little angels wild!

March 11

IT STARTED WITH THE GREEKS!

Greek physician Aesculapius,
Who lived more than 1000 years BC,
Originated the concept of extracting diseased teeth,
And thus began a three-millennium pulling spree!

March 12

REPRODUCTIVE FRENZY

Your recently food-filled mouth provides
a warm, wet, nutrient-rich environment for germs;

In just 20 minutes, a single bacterium can divide in two.

In other words, that hyperactive cootie can generate
more than *16 million* progeny in just 8 hours!

Is it any wonder dentists encourage
brushing and flossing right after you chew?

March 13

WHERE THE SMELL BEGINS

Where does bad breath come from?

When those oral bacteria go to the bathroom in your mouth,

Their waste includes a variety of chemicals called VSCs,

Volatile Sulfur (like in rotten eggs) Compounds,
making all your friends head South!

March 14

HALITOSIS HOTEL

The real estate VSC-generating bacteria prefer to call home

Is far on the back of your tongue;

That's why tongue-scrapers are recommended

If you don't want your breath smelling like dung!

March 15

Matrimonial Brouhaha

In the Talmud, a collection of ancient writings
Upon which the Jewish faith is based,
Bad breath is considered a serious ailment;
It even represents grounds for a divorce case!

March 16

Interproximal Residue

See a friend with food stuck in their teeth?
Try giving these Aussie-favorites a whack:
Carnivore: "Hey mate,
you still got meat on your grill!"
Vegetarian: "Hey mate,
you still got spice in your rack!"

March 17

DDS or DMD?

DMD stands for *Dentariae Medicinae Doctorae*
(first awarded by the Harvard School of Dental Medicine,
the first university-affiliated dental institution),
And DDS stands for Doctor of Dental Surgery.
Academic requirements for the two degrees—now set
by the American Dental Association—are identical.
Degree citations are up to the school,
and so ends this mystery.

March 18

PIG LATIN

In the olden days of sailing ships,
Voyages often ran long and cuisine was not Zagat.
That's when gristly salt pork filled sailors' bellies
And grousing about rations was "chewing the fat."

March 19

LATE NOSH!

In ancient Egypt, the well-documented
"Opening of the Mouth" ritual
Was conducted as part of the funeral
of a mummified dignitary
In the belief this would enable the deceased to see,
smell, breathe, hear, drink, and *eat* in the afterlife
And thus enjoy, and be nourished by, the beverage
and food offerings brought to the tomb—post funerary.

March 20

NEVER A PATIENT COMPLAINT!

At numerous burial
sites, archeologists have
found in mummified skulls
Dental bridges—held in place
with fine gold strands, carefully wired.
It seems reasonable to assume, given the
significance of the Opening of the Mouth ritual,
That the embalmers wanted their subjects to have
full sets of teeth—installed posthumously, if necessary—
with which to enjoy offerings made to the recently expired.

March 21

MIDNIGHT RIDER

Paul Revere's talents as a silversmith and patriot
Are revered by one and all.
But did you know he was also a dentist?
For a revolutionary toothache,
Paul was the man to call.

March 22

WAAAAAAAAAAY BEFORE CSI

Silversmith Paul Revere is the first person on record to successfully employ dental forensics in America.

In 1775, Revere crafted a silver-wire fixed bridge for Continental Army Major General Joseph Warren, making use of his modest dental knowledge.

Not long after, the General was killed in the Battle of Bunker Hill where his insignia-free body was hastily buried in an unmarked mass grave.

A year later, Warren's remains were exhumed, and Revere easily identified the man by his bridge.

[N.B. Why were the General's insignia removed? The retreating Colonials didn't want the British to discover that a high-ranking officer was among the casualties.]

March 23

FRIAR PLUCK

Brother Giovanni Battista Osengio of Italy,
Between 1868 and 1904—a mere 36 years,
Did extract more than two million teeth.
Think that's a lot? Don't even try counting the tears.

March 24

A MATTER OF CHOICE

Some weird conversations occur in the dental office,
Here's one that might make you laugh...or weep:
"Hey Doc, do I have to floss *all* my teeth?"
"No, Tommy, just the ones you want to keep."

March 25

GRIM USE FOR X-RAYS

Like fingerprints and DNA, everyone's teeth are unique—
even those of "identical" twins;

That's why dental records are so useful in forensic work.

(Lots more folks have dental x-rays on file
than a record of their DNA!)

Even if a body is burned or decomposed,
the teeth tell the tale; just ask any coroner's clerk.

March 26

PARTIAL EXPLANATION

Sally has "Summer Teeth":

Summer here, summer there,

Summer in her pocket,

And others are in her mouth, that's where.

March 27

GAPOSIS

Got a space between your teeth?

If so, you suffer from "diastema" [say di-a-*ste*-ma].

The word comes from Old Latin—Early Italian!

It means "to separate,"—*Mama Mia!*

March 28

NO TERMITES HERE

George Washington's teeth were *never* made of wood;
One set of his dentures was constructed
of hippopotamus ivory and gold.
Made by John Greenwood,
a prominent dentist at the time,
These hinged, spring-loaded plates
were a marvel to behold!

[N.B. The springs forced the top plate up against the palate when George opened his mouth to eat or speak.]

March 29

WOODEN DENTURES

The innocent-sounding phrase,
"My back teeth are floating,"
is a curious reference—
A genteel allusion—
to the uncomfortably large liquid volume
Occupying the speaker's
distended bladder—immense.

[N.B. According to Drs. N. Moriyama and M. Hasegawa, as reported in the April 1987 *Bulletin of the History of Dentistry*, in the early 16th Century the Japanese were making full upper and lower *wooden* denture bases to which prosthetic front teeth of ivory were attached. An array of round nail heads in the rear took care of the chewing normally handled by molars.]

March 30

THE TREADLE DRILL

The principle of removing decayed tissue with a drill
was understood from ancient times.

Getting the drill *bit*—called a *bur* [with only one *r*]—to
spin *rapidly* had inspired solutions best described as *crude*.

In 1790, Dr. John Greenwood adapted
his mother's foot-treadle spinning wheel to turn the drill.

That inventive Greenwood was obviously one sharp dude!

March 31

IN THE PINK

There's one sure way to tell
if you're brushing and flossing well.

Pick up "disclosing tablets" and a cheap dental mirror
from your local pharmacy;

Chew the tablets, swish, spit, and peek at the reflection;

Wherever your teeth are pink,
the presence of plaque will be plain to see.

[N.B. Some members of the hip generation refer
to plaque as "gum scum," an appropriately
colorful allusion. In any event, be sure to brush
your teeth again *after* using the disclosing tablets.]

APRIL

April 1

OPERATORY CONVERSATION

"Sally, are you going to put the baby tooth we just removed under your pillow tonight?"

Shaking her head no, Sally says, "Unh, unh, Doctor Tunney."

"Why not?"

"Easter is just a couple days away; I'm gonna put it under my pillow with some carrots Saturday night so the Tooth Fairy can feed the Easter Bunny."

April 2

A BALTIMORE MUST-SEE

In 1996, The Dr. Samuel D. Harris
National Museum of Dentistry

In association with the Smithsonian Institution

Formally opened in downtown Baltimore, Maryland.

As Michigan pediatric dentist Harris
cut the "dental floss ribbon," one of his
lifelong dreams was brought to fruition.

April 3

DENTAL EDUTAINMENT

A favorite with schoolchildren and adults alike,

The NMD's exhibits include George Washington's dentures,

Queen Victoria's dental instruments,

And the world's only mouth-shaped jukebox—
fascinating adventures!

[N.B. Be sure not to miss the newest addition,
Saliva: A Remarkable Fluid, the first in a planned
three-part exhibition, *Your Spitting Image*.]

April 4

MOST VALUABLE TOOTH

We thank the *Guinness Book of World Records* for this one:

In 1816, a tooth belonging to renowned scientist
Sir Isaac (1642-1727) Newton

Was sold in London for £730 (equivalent to $3,241 today).

It was purchased by a nobleman who had it set in a ring.
Who gives a fig?

April 5

MANHATTAN COWBOY

Pearl Gray was a New York dentist
In 1904, his day job he did quit.
Then he changed his first name to Zane,
Wrote 60 Westerns, and became quite a hit!

[N.B. Zane Gray's *Riders of the Purple Sage* sold 2,000,000+ copies and was filmed three times. Unable to find a publisher for his first book, he used his own money to have it printed.]

April 6

TOOTH RITE

For centuries, Brits believed mice had magical powers.
Baby teeth were dropped into the nearest mouse hole
While a prayer was said asking that the donating child would enjoy a toothache-free life;
That's one way of fulfilling the parental role.

April 7

PORTERHOUSE, NEW YORK, T-BONE, FILET MIGNON, OR GROUND ROUND?

One-hundred years ago, half of America's adults over 65 were toothless.

Today, less than 10% suffer that calamity.

The average American with a full set of teeth can exert bite pressure of 30-40 pounds per square inch while the average denture-wearer can only exert about 15.

Soooooooooooo, if you want to celebrate *your* 65th with a juicy steak dinner, brush and floss with assiduity!

April 8

THE MICRO-AIR ABRASION DRILL

This device is a non-drill tissue excavator;

It operates like a mini-sandblaster
and is best for cavities that are not too deep.

A high-speed jet of compressed gas pumps
a thin stream of grit at the diseased part of the tooth.

The debris is suctioned away;
that's the stuff you don't want to keep.

April 9

THE AIRY UPSIDE

Air abrasion generates no heat, removes minimal tissue,

And rarely requires anesthetic
except for those squeamish in the extreme.

It produces a very smooth surface, ideal for composite fillings;

And most patients rate this technique absolutely supreme!

April 10

AUDIO PERSUASION

Can't get your kids to brush and floss?

Then try serenading them, mom,

With a dental drill sound effects clip

From audiosparx.com.

April 11

DO THE MATH

Dental research is a marvelous thing;
It teaches us much that's worthwhile,
For instance, it takes 43 muscles to frown,
But only 17 muscles to smile.

April 12

TUSCAN LEGACY

Long before the Romans
In the 7th and 6th centuries BC
Tuscany was the land of the Etruscans,
Home of Etruscan *dentistry.*

April 13

THE FIRST PARTIALS

Using animal and human tooth replacements,
plus carvings of ivory and bone,
Etruscan craftsmen prepared
the world's first-known dental prosthetics
Which they attached to nearby choppers with gold bands,
Creating—for their day-and-time—a very pleasing aesthetic.

April 14

DENTAL LIT AND *PRO BONO* PIONEER

The first dental book published (*self*-published) in America
Was the 1801, 26-page *Treatise on the Human Teeth*
by New York dentist Dr. Richard Cortland Skinner.
He was also the first to establish an in-hospital dental clinic
And a dental facility for treating the poor without charge
(but the services did not include a free dinner).

April 15

GOT ROT?

Upon the introduction of refined sugar to 1500s Europe,
Dental caries quickly did skyrocket.
At the time, only the wealthy could afford this new import
So *they* of the deep pockets were the privileged,
adventuresome, and first-in-line to experience
many an empty tooth socket.

April 16

WHITE SUGAR—BLACK TEETH

In John Strype's *Life of Bishop Aylmer* published in 1701,
We learn that the insatiable sweet tooth of
Queen Elizabeth I rewarded her with hideous, black decay.
Late one night she had a toothache so excruciating
that court physicians were summoned.
When extraction of the painful molar was suggested,
fearful Liz demanded they come back another day.

April 17

FOR CROWN AND COUNTRY

On that occasion, Aylmer, aged Bishop of London,
was among those attending the Queen.
To allay fear in his liege, occupant of the throne,
And demonstrate that her concern was unwarranted,
He sacrificed for extraction, then and there,
a tooth (probably decayed) of his very own!

April 18

THE GREAT MASTICATOR

"Chew each bite 50 to 100 times,"
your parents advised,
It will aid mightily in your digestion."
Early 20th-century foodie Horace Fletcher
was the daddy of this notion,
And Corn Flake King, Dr. John Harvey Kellogg,
helped publicize the suggestion.

April 19

EARLY MIDDLE AGES

In the period 500-1000 AD,
The best-educated Europeans
could be found in the priesthood.
Whether you needed confessing,
doctoring, or *dentisting,*
An officer of the Church could help
your mind, body, and mouth feel good.

April 20

GIDDY STUFF

In 1844, Boston dentist Horace Wells and his neighbor
Bought tickets for an evening's entertainment
to relieve boredom and strain.
The host of the affair invited audience members (including
Wells's neighbor) to sniff nitrous oxide (laughing gas),
And soon, Wells's friend got high, stumbled, cut his shin
badly on a bench, but told the doc he was feeling no pain.

April 21

MAKING HISTORY

The very next day in his office,
Wells assembled a cast of three:

The previous evening's nitrous oxide host,

A fellow dentist named Riggs, and himself.

Wells then received a large dose of laughing gas (rendering him unconscious), Dr. Riggs pulled one of Wells's teeth; and when the gas wore off, the willing patient reported that he had felt no pain—cause for a major toast!

[N.B. After this experiment, Wells commenced the regular use of nitrous oxide with his extraction patients. Today, Wells—not Morton or Jackson to be discussed below—is credited by the medical profession as the "Father of Anesthesia" for his pioneering work in the field.]

April 22

HIGHER AND HIGHER

The modest effectiveness of *nitrous oxide* as a painkiller

Was not lost on one William Thomas Green Morton,
a mediocre student and protégé of Wells.

Soon afterward, Morton discovered
that local physician-chemist Charles T. Jackson

Was studying the anesthetic properties of *diethyl ether*,
another gas for inducing patient spells.

April 23

WHO'S ON FIRST?

Morton snooped around Jackson's facility and conferred with the proprietor before making a modest purchase.

While there, he quickly concluded that *ether* could be far more potent than *laughing gas*.

Returning to his own practice, Morton successfully used ether on a dental patient—a test run,

Before inviting a member of the press to *document* his next procedure—*that* took some ego-driven brass!

[N.B. It was 1846 when Dr. Oliver Wendell Holmes recommended, in a letter to Morton, that the term "anesthesia" be employed to describe the medium that renders patients insensitive to pain. Holmes later became Dean of the Harvard Medical School.]

April 24

FIFTY-FIFTY

C.T. Jackson was a brilliant inventor, but he rarely publicized his discoveries;

He even accused Samuel F.B. Morse of stealing the telegraph invention from him—truly a shame;

And, of course, C.T. brought suit for theft of the ether application after Morton publicly demonstrated its use.

Jackson and Morton were profoundly unhappy when the court of public opinion declared they should *share* the financial rewards *and* the fame.

[N.B. Years later, while in a chloroform-induced stupor, Wells performed a criminal act, was arrested and held overnight in jail where he committed suicide. Morton died penniless. Jackson died in an insane asylum.]

April 25

TODAY, IT'S CALLED "NOSE CANDY"

As dental science improved and professional standards were established in the mid-1800s,

Burgeoning public demand for oral care brought people to the office in sunshine or rain.

Some, however—the die-hard dentalphobics—stayed away due to fear of pain.

The commonly-dispensed anesthetic provided to this squeamish clientele? *Cocaine!*

April 26

"NEW" COCAINE

Ultimately, the addictive properties of cocaine demanded the introduction of

An equally effective, but *non-addictive,* replacement to dull the pain.

In 1905, German chemist Alfred Einhorn discovered the perfect substitute: "*pro*caine"

And gave it the trade name "Novocain" from the Latin *novus* (new) plus cocaine.

April 27

RED ZONE

Italian tomato pie is best with mozzarella;
Fresh out of the oven, it's impossible to resist.
But when piping-hot cheese hits the roof of your mouth
"Pizza Palate" feels like you got smashed with a fist!

April 28

PAINLESS PARKER

Colorful and outrageous Dr. Edgar R.R. Parker,
a graduate of the Philadelphia Dental College,

Ran a 30-office practice on the West Coast a
century ago, earning him both money and fame.

When a new California law said
dentists couldn't operate under a "false ID,"

"Painless" Parker went to court...
and legally adopted that colorful first name.

April 29

STICKS AND STONES

As a stunt, "Painless Parker"
made 357 extractions in one day;

He then *strung* the teeth and wore them as a necklace.

Some detractors called him
a disgrace to the profession;

Others called him dangerous and reckless.

April 30

LIKELY COMMENT BY A DOC PARKER PATIENT

There are tortures that are *physical,*

And there are tortures that are *mental;*

But the worst torture of all is *both:*

It's an appointment with *Painless Parker Dental!*

[N.B. Painless Parker died in 1952 at the ripe old age of 80.
Practice consultant Rosemary Bray provided this quatrain.]

MAY

May 1

AMERICA'S FIRST WOMAN DENTIST

Emeline Roberts Jones learned how to drill and fill teeth alongside her dentist-husband.

Upon his death in 1885, Emeline became the first woman to travel from town to town with a portable dentist's chair.

In time, she was accepted into both the Connecticut State Dental Society and the National Dental Association.

For almost half-a-century, the people of eastern Connecticut and Rhode Island benefited from her care.

May 2

TEETH CLEANING

The tartar- and plaque-removal procedure
administered by today's skilled dental hygienist

Is technically referred to as a *prophylaxis*,
from the Greek for "an advance guard."

Not only does a "prophy" clean up what
you've missed with your toothbrush and floss,

It helps prevent gum disease that can lead to serious
heart problems—like arteries that become hard.

May 3

ASSEMBLY LINE BRUSHES

The Florence Manufacturing Company
of Massachusetts was founded in 1866

And for many years produced a line of brushes using
the "Florence Compound," a primitive plastic.

FMC's mass-produced items included hair, scrub,
shaving lather, and toilet brushes.

In 1884, at the suggestion of New York dentist Dr. Meyer
Rhein, the company developed the world's first mass-
produced *tooth*brush trade-named the "Pro-phy-lac-tic."

May 4

PACKAGING TRENDSETTER

Toothbrushes produced by FMC's competition
were all handmade, one at a time.

Not only was the Pro-phy-lac-tic brush
(dubbed the "Pro-Brush") mass-produced,

Each one was packaged in its own cute little box—
a sanitary and historical *first*!

The packaging alone was a major hygienic
innovation that gave sales a huge boost.

May 5

SOFTIE

The advent of mass-produced toothbrushes
heralded a new era;

The toothpick, America's previous favorite
for personal oral hygiene, was upstaged.

With the introduction of DuPont's
softer nylon bristles just before WWII,

Enthusiasm for the "new-and-improved,"
gum-friendly brush raged and raged.

May 6

MAN'S FIRST BAD HABIT?

The skulls of Neanderthals show grooves
between the teeth in close proximity to the jawbone.

Common sense says that these could only have
been caused by the frequent use of toothpicks.

While we can merely speculate as to what material was
employed, wooden splinters, fish bones, ivory, shells,
porcupine quills, and, yes, *bird claws* come to mind.

Even with modern man,
the toothpick habit is a hard one to kick!

[N.B. Source, *Smithsonian Magazine,* January 1997:
Q: What is the oldest empirically documented human habit?
A: Picking one's teeth.]

May 7

WORLD TOUR

In 1907, while sailing in the South Pacific

Aboard his good ship Snark,

Author Jack London visited the Marquesas Islands,

Where he and his crew did park.

May 8

Good Samaritan

Soon after arriving, London encountered
An aged Chinaman, tormented by awful ache.
Recalling the forceps in his medical kit,
London offered the errant tooth to take.

May 9

Amateur Dentist

In excruciating pain, and with no other option,
The terrified, wiggly-toothed patient agreed to submit.
With ease, London completed the extraction,
The Oriental was relieved,
and Jack's pride swelled without limit.

May 10

Gilbert and Sullivan on Amateur Dentistry

The advertising quack who wearies
With tales of countless cures,
His teeth, I've enacted, Shall all be extracted
By terrified amateurs.

[N.B. These lines appear here through the genius
of *The Mikado* (1855) lyricist William S. Gilbert.]

May 11

DENTURE PERMIT

In Vermont, a pre-suffrage state law remains on the books:
Women must obtain their husband's written permission
Before being fitted with false teeth.
Sounds to me like a matter for the next ballot proposition.

May 12

SAME WORD, DIFFERENT MEANINGS

A *plaque* is a flat plate, usually rectangular, that is mounted on a wall or monument to display information.

The images on a plaque are usually engraved or embossed.

In your mouth, plaque is a film of mucus and bacteria that constantly forms on your teeth;

It can easily be removed if you regularly brush and floss.

May 13

VINTAGE MATH

Tartar is a reddish acid compound in the juice of grapes that gets deposited on the inside of casks during winemaking.

Calculus is a branch of mathematics, the dictionary tells us.

When plaque, the icky kind in your mouth, is allowed to accumulate through the neglect of oral hygiene, it becomes a hard yellowish-green deposit—really yucky— that includes various salts such as calcium carbonate.

Here's the punch line: That hard stuff (It has to be *scraped* off by a dental hygienist!) is called *tartar* or *calculus*!

May 14

THAT'S D-I-S-G-U-S-T-I-N-G!

We're not done yet!

That calculus or tartar?

It's the *same stuff* from which your body makes *gallstones* and *kidney stones!*

And IT'S ON *YOUR* TEETH unless, than the too-lazy-to-brush, you are smarter!

May 15

TOOTH QUIZ CRAM

It was John Hunter, a British cabinet maker who made a
career change and later became surgeon to King George III,

Who wrote *The Natural History of Teeth* in 1771 and
named the various types (from front to back)
so everyone would have ease in finding:

Their *incisors* (four pairs used for cutting),
cuspids (two pairs used for tearing),

Bicuspids (four pairs used for crushing),
and *molars* (four pairs—or trios
when there are *wisdom teeth*—used for grinding).

May 16

TOOTH GEOGRAPHY

The contact surface of your bicuspids
and molars is called *occlusal*,

While the surfaces facing adjacent teeth are *proximal*;

The tongue-side is *lingual* and the cheek-side is *buccal*.

These Latin-based terms are a *delight*
to every Scrabble-playing animal.

May 17

WAIT, THERE'S MORE!

The surface of a tooth *closest* to the *middle*
of your *front* teeth is called *mesial*,

And that *furthest* from the *middle* is called *distal*.

Now that our little lesson is over,

Everything should be clear as crystal.

May 18

BENT?

There's nothing attractive about crooked teeth;

For thousands of years,
folks have attempted to straighten them.

As far back as 400 BC, Hippocrates,
Greek "Father of Medicine,"

The sad fate of his orthodontically-
challenged colleagues did condemn.

May 19

ETYMOLOGY

Making up new words has got to be a hoot!

In 1841, a Frenchman named Lafoulon added to our
lexicon the designation "orthodontia"—newly minted.

Soon afterward, J.M. Alexis Schange—
Parisian inventor of tooth-straightening bands—

Wrote a landmark book on malocclusion (bad bite)
in which the new term was first printed.

May 20

ORTHODONTICS

The menu of orthodontic problems is extensive:

Crossbite; protruding, crooked, or misaligned teeth;
sleep apnea (interrupted breathing, snoring);

Tooth grinding (bruxism); protruding or retruding jaw;
speech impairment; and TMJ dislocation.

With solutions offered by your friendly orthodontist, praise
from your beautiful new mouth will soon be pouring.

EDWARD HARTLEY ANGLE (1855-1930)

May 21

FATHER OF ORTHODONTICS

There are two other well-qualified contenders for this title,
Norman W. Kingsley and J.N. Farrar by name,
But it is Edward H. Angle whom *today's* orthodontists
For this honor most vigorously proclaim.

May 22

THE EARLY YEARS

Born on a Pennsylvania farm—the fifth of seven kids,
And not overly fond of what he called "book learnin',"
Angle delighted in improving and
creating mechanical farm equipment;
It was *simplicity of design*
for which he was always yearnin'.

May 23

QUICK STUDY

At eighteen,
Angle was apprenticed to a dentist who was a family friend.
At nineteen,
in the Pennsylvania College of Dentistry he did enroll.
A year-and-a-half later—it was 1876, Angle graduated
And entered general practice to continue pursuit of his goal.

May 24

DENTAL IMPRESSIONS

While a student at PCD, mechanically-gifted Angle
attended just two lectures on orthodontics.
[That was everything the curriculum offered on this subject!]
But those sessions were all it took for Angle to get infected;
To be an orthodontist was the career he did elect!

May 25

A CRUSHING OBSESSION

Now, take a peek at Angle's no-nonsense likeness
[May 21] and ask yourself this question:
"Does this look like a man whose lifelong ambition
was pursuing the beautiful smiles illusion?"
"No!" should be your resounding response.
It was all about the BITE—what dental pros call *occlusion*!

May 26

It's Included in the Price

The simple fact is, straight teeth fit together properly,
Thus enabling people to chew their food without discomfort.

Straight teeth also reduce wear and tear on the *temporomandibular joint* (TMJ)—where your jaws hinge!

It's all as simple as that; a beautiful smile is the *bonus* you get from your hardworking orthodontist's effort.

May 27

The Orthodontist's Bible

Having said all that, you won't be surprised to learn about
Malocclusion of the Teeth, Angle's landmark composition

In which he set forth the *first* simple and logical classification system for malocclusion—still in use today.

With all the innovation in orthodontics he inspired, and to keep his book current while it remained in print, Angle's opus reached, in 1907, its 628-page *seventh* edition.

May 28

Inspired Alumni

In 1900, Angle founded the world's *first* school of orthodontia in St. Louis, Missouri.

His passion moved graduates of that first class in 1901 to organize The Society of Orthodontists

Which, in 1902, was renamed The *American* Society of Orthodontists

And has developed into the present 15,000-member American Association of Orthodontists.

May 29

ORTHODONTIC GENEALOGY

Chances are the AAO orthodontist you're seeing today
Was trained by an orthodontist
who was trained by an orthodontist
Who was trained by an orthodontist
who was *personally* trained by Edward H. Angle,
And that indisputably confirms Angle's place at the *top*
of the "Father of Orthodontics" paternity candidate list!

May 30

THUMBSUCKERS, LISTEN UP!

Once permanent teeth begin to erupt, thumbsucking can:
Narrow the *upper* jaw and cause "buck teeth"
(when the top front teeth develop gaps and flare).
Cause the *lower* front teeth
to push back toward the tongue.
Sooooooooo, take your thumbsucker to the dentist
before the damage is done—unless you plan
a major investment in future orthodontic care.

May 31

VOCABULARY LESSON

The fun word for today is "snaggletooth."
It's a tooth that's broken or out of alignment.
Betcha can't say the word without smiling;
That's today's most challenging assignment.

JUNE

June 1

Aerial Artist

1950s film icon James Byron Dean was an
outstanding high school drama student and athlete.

Sadly, one day, all his front teeth were knocked out
while he practiced gymnastics on the trapeze.

If you see his performances in *East of Eden*,
Rebel without a Cause, or *Giant*,

Look closely for his bridgework;
and be glad the script didn't require him to sneeze.

June 2

TWILIGHT ZONE STUFF

James Dean was born on February 8, 1931,
in Marion, Indiana,

The son of Winton and Mildred (Wilson) Dean;

His mother passed away when he was six.

James's father was a *dental lab technician*;
who knew his son would make it BIG
while wearing dentures on the silver screen?

June 3

COMBAT-READY

It's hard to function in battle
if you're the prisoner of a throbbing toothache.

During World War II, the U.S. Army imposed dental
hygiene standards that were drill sergeant tough.

When our troops returned, the American
market for toothpowder, toothpaste,
toothbrushes, and mouthwash exploded;

We just couldn't get enough of the stuff!

June 4

THE FIRST ANESTHETIC

In olden times when the only relief for
serious toothache was extraction,
A major dilemma faced the man with the tongs:
If the offending molar was badly decayed,
The procedure was begun
with booze and rowdy songs.

June 5

NOW *THAT'S* A TEMPORARY!

If decay had reduced the tooth to a shell,
A *filling* (tiny pebbles, lead, resin, what have you)
was used to reinforce the sucker;
Otherwise the shell would be crushed during removal,
And that would make *both* ends of the patient pucker!

[N.B. It was Roman physician Cornelius Celsus who,
sometime in the 1st Century AD, recommended
this procedure for removing badly rotted teeth.]

June 6

OBJET D'ART

Enamel is a vitreous composition, usually opaque,
and is often applied at very high temps

To the surface of metal, glass, or pottery
by talented artisans—either *clothed* or *in the buff*.

For centuries, from Asia to Europe,

Jewelry and other works of art were,
and still are, often decorated with the stuff.

June 7

VOILÀ!

In the decades following publication of
Pierre Fauchard's *Le chirurgien dentiste*

Innovations in French dentistry
proceeded at a remarkable pace.

Dental prosthetics (false teeth, dentures, bridges, etc.)
of gold became quite common.

Sooooooooo, in 1746, Dr. Claude Mouton got into the
history books by recommending, for the first time,
white enameling on *gold crowns* for a more esthetic face.

[N.B. I don't speak French, so I looked it up:
The English translation for "voilà" is "lo and behold."]

June 8

THE PRICE OF MATERNITY

The centuries-old wives tale,

"For every child the mother loses a tooth,"

Flies in the face of what we now know

About the *real* causes of tooth loss—the *truth*!

June 9

DING DONGS AND TWINKIES

New York University College of Dentistry's
Dr. Stefanie Russell sheds new light on this troubling matter.
Her study of 2,635 women concludes that mothers
burdened with the time-consuming demands of childcare
Are more likely than their childless counterparts
to neglect their oral hygiene and eat the same
junk food as their kids—including *cookie batter!*

[N.B. Michael F. Roizen, MD, co-author of *You: The Owner's Manual,* states that gingivitis in pregnant women contributes to increased risk of miscarriage and low birth weight babies. Clearly, regular dental checkups are even more important for pregnant women than the rest of us.]

June 10

STARRY-EYED

Born in 1866 to immigrants from Luxembourg,
The boy was youngest in a family of eight.
He loved American history...and *especially* our flag;
For him, June 14 was an all-important calendar date!

June 11

BIRTH OF OLD GLORY

For on that day in 1777,
The Continental Congress reviewed the efforts of
Elizabeth (Betsy) Griscom Ross.
Her design of the Stars-and-Stripes was approved
Faster than you can say "dental floss."

June 12

MULTI-TASKER

So he could pay
Lake Forest College of Dentistry tuition,
At nineteen, our young man sold books door-to-door,
And taught at Wisconsin's Stony Hill School
[where he initiated the first Flag Day celebration];
Who could possibly ask for more?

[N.B. Our distinguished honoree, who will be
named in the June 14 quatrain below,
graduated *first* in his dental school class!]

June 13

RELENTLESS

When organizing flag-honoring celebrations
all across the country
For the next 31 years,
this human dynamo never failed to find a way.
In 1916, President Woodrow Wilson made it official,
And inaugurated June 14 as National Flag Day.

BERNARD J. CIGRAND (1866-1932)

June 14

WE SALUTE OUR FLAG *AND* WE SALUTE THIS MAN!

Thus we see the culmination
Of a young schoolteacher's early obsession.
He ultimately became a dentist
and Dean of the Illinois School of Dentistry.
Congratulations, Dr. Bernard J. Cigrand;
you conferred great honor upon your profession.

June 15

AMERICAN GOTHIC

The famous Grant Wood painting
Of a spinster and her pitchfork-wielding dad
Used the artist's *sister* as the female model
And his *dentist* as the farmer-in-overalls-clad.

[N.B. Grant Wood's dentist was Dr. B.H. McKeeby.]

June 16

DENTAL CHAIRS

We told you about the *bad* old days when patient and dentist interacted on knotted floorboards.

While this was uncomfortable for the patient whose clinical session was mercifully brief,

Consider the physical toll these awkward positions took on the poor doctor;

By end of day, his back had to be in knots, bringing all kinds of muscle-cramp grief!

[N.B. Was this the marketing opportunity that launched the chiropractic profession? Maybe not; but it's an intriguing line of thought—and possibly another book!]

June 17

WINDSOR CHAIR MAKEOVER

Josiah Foster Flagg (1763-1816)
Was America's first full-time dentist, native-born, and—befitting his status—usually well dressed.
He is credited with inventing the first dental chair in 1790
Featuring two key innovations: an extended armrest for holding instruments and an *adjustable* headrest.

June 18

LA-Z-BOY PRECURSOR?

In 1832, Dr. James Snell, British author of the *Practical Guide to Operations on the Teeth*
And "Member of the Royal College of Surgeons," as well as being a fine
"Lecturer on the Anatomy and Diseases of the Teeth, &c. &c. &c."
Invented the first dental chair that could *recline!*

[N.B. Text in quotation marks is taken verbatim from the cover of an original copy of Dr. Snell's book.]

June 19

LOOKIN' UP

In 1848, Milton Waldo Hanchett of Syracuse, NY
Patented the first *modern* dental chair
with features like these:
A headrest, a *height-adjustable seat*, and a back
That could be tilted to put the
patient *and* dentist at ease.

June 20

HANG IN THERE!

In 1877, Professor Basil Manly Wilkerson, DDS, MD,
Introduced the first model of "The Wilkerson Chair"
featuring an up-and-down trajectory;
It was the world's first, pump-type *hydraulic* dental chair.
Wilkerson's many inventions
also included a scrotal suspensory.

[N.B.1. The first Wilkerson Chair was marketed at $175.]

[N.B.2. A scrotal suspensory is an athletic supporter;
in the vernacular, it's called a *jock strap!*]

June 21

A FRIEND'S TRIBUTE

"He was the most skillful gambler, and the nerviest,
Fastest, deadliest man with a six-gun I ever saw."
So proclaimed OK Corral shootout partner, Wyatt Earp.
The fact Holliday was also a *dentist* who knew how to "drill"
more than just teeth, puts most folks in total awe!

[N.B. Doc Holliday was born with a cleft palate and a hare lip. At the age of eight weeks, the child's deformities were repaired by his surgeon-uncle, Dr. John McKey. Could it be that Holliday wore that huge handlebar mustache to hide his hare lip?]

June 22

DENTAL SCHOOL

John was born to Henry and Alice Holliday
in Griffin, Georgia, on August 14, 1851.

After the Civil War, he spent his youth
on a 2,450 acre farm where mastering the pistol
was a hobby for which he had time aplenty.

With admirable intentions, John's father sent his
already-well-educated son to study at the Pennsylvania
College of Dental Surgery in his eighteenth year.

In Philadelphia, young Holliday spent his evenings
in red-light district gambling halls, but nevertheless
managed to graduate near the top of the class
with his DDS degree at age twenty.

JOHN HENRY "DOC" HOLLIDAY (1851-1887)

June 23

HOPES DASHED

Upon his return to Georgia, John joined the
Atlanta dental practice of Dr. Arthur C. Ford;

But a short time later Holliday was diagnosed with
tuberculosis (the same illness that killed his mother
when he was only fifteen) in a highly-advanced state.

Searching for a warmer, drier climate—
and an eagerly-desired postponement of his demise,

John headed for Dallas, where he would seek his fate.

June 24

POKER AND FARO

Upon arriving in "the Big D," Holliday joined
the practice of Dr. John A. Seegar,

But the new dentist's frequent, mid-procedure
coughing bouts sent patients scrambling.

Frequently absent from the office,

Holliday met his financial needs with the
second revenue-generating skill he had
perfected in Philadelphia: gambling.

June 25

ADIOS, DOC

If you Google Doc Holliday, you'll be rewarded
with more than *eighteen million* hits!

Googling Pierre Fauchard,
the French "Father of Modern Dentistry,"
garners fewer than *eighty thousand.*

Holliday, who died in bed at a Colorado health spa
at age 36 after enjoying a palliative glass of whiskey,

Is unquestionably the most famous/infamous
dentist ever to live in this—or any other—land.

June 26

IN THE DNA

Dr. Robert A. Holliday,

Dr. John Henry Holliday's cousin in the gene pool,

Was the prime mover

In establishing Georgia's first dental school.

June 27

MEET ALEX TREBEK

Know what the "alveolar socket" is?

That's the peculiar name for the holes
in your jaw in which your teeth rest.

With the standard set of 32 choppers in your head,
that means you have 32 alveolar sockets.

This kind of knowledge might land you a spot on
"Jeopardy!" where you could compete with the best.

June 28

SACRILEGIOUS EPITHET?

A patient in the dental reception area

Heard shortly after her arrival

The emphatically-enunciated word, *"Jesus!"*

Come from inside the office at irregular intervals.

June 29

SATISFACTION ANTICIPATION

Convinced the poor victim was being tortured
The patient resolved to have her curiosity purged.
In due course, the operatory door opened
And a well-known man-of-the-cloth emerged.

June 30

RESOLUTION

A short time later,
The dentist relieved his curious patient's concerns;
Turns out the minister's dentures required adjustment
So he wouldn't *hiss* excessively
while delivering Sunday sermons.

[N.B. For more delightful anecdotes from
author Susan Lawrence Oliver, get your hands
on a copy of *Reminiscences of a Bostonian* (1952).]

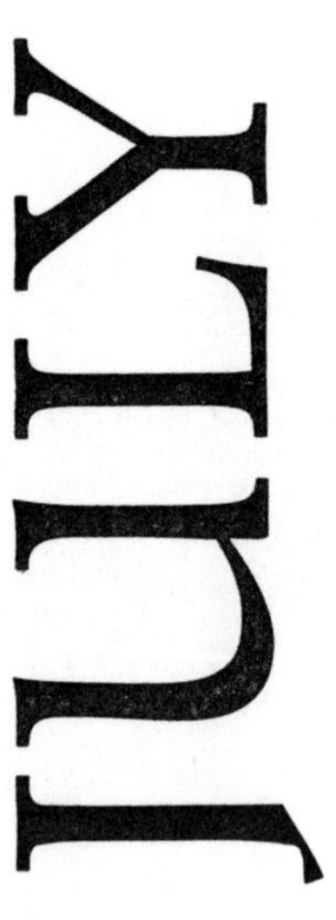
JULY

July 1

IT'S NOT THE WHITE, FLUFFY STUFF

For more than 2,000 years,
its roots and leaves have found medicinal use.

In case you didn't know it,
marshmallow is a perennial herb.

The prestigious *British Herbal Compendium* indicates
that marshmallow mouthwash or gargle
will soothe the mouth and throat.

We recommend you try it, old chap; it's simply superb!

July 2

SOAK IN SALT WATER

Misplaced dentures are a common problem;
Loss while swimming is a major cause.
With all those seniors living in Florida,
Denture-strewn beaches
can give a person pause.

July 3

FULL HOUSE

President Thomas Jefferson
Died at 83 of a natural cause.
On the occasion of his passing,
A full set of teeth still occupied his jaws.

July 4

EMPTY SOCKETS

At the age of 90, also of natural cause,
President John Adams was dead.
On the occasion of his passing,
There wasn't a single tooth in the poor man's head.

[N.B. Thomas Jefferson died on July 4, 1826,
just a few hours before his compatriot, John Adams.
*That day marked the 50th anniversary of the
first signing of the Declaration of Independence!*]

July 5

FAST CURRICULUM

In 1923, London (England) dentist Alfred Moss
Took advanced classes at the Indiana Dental College,
But spent most of his time at the track
Practicing—not dentistry—but for *Indy 500* knowledge!

July 6

AHHHHHHHH, THE CHECKERED FLAG!

Moss qualified for a spot in the 1924 race
Starting in 20th position and finishing at 16—
that's no crime!
His purse was $900,
A respectable sum at the time.

[N.B. Sterling Moss, son of the above-named Alfred Moss, is a member of the Grand Prix Hall of Fame.]

July 7

PLAQUE-WORTHY PERFORMANCE

On and off the track,
the Indiana University School of Dentistry
Continues to produce professionals who show no fear.
Jack Miller, DDS '92—known as the
Indy 500's "Racing Dentist,"
Started at 17th position and finished at 20th
in his 1977 rookie year.

[N.B. Miller drove a Crest Racing Dallara/Infiniti for primary sponsor Proctor & Gamble; his purse: $171,250!]

July 8

ENAMEL SCABBARD

The pirate, swinging from a boarding rope with one hand,
And brandishing a pistol with the other,
Clenches a knife in his jaws—he's "armed to the teeth."
Now hurry;
share this toothsome bit of trivia with your mother.

[N.B. This phrase was first used by
British Lord Richard Cobden in 1849.]

July 9

ONE FOR THE RECORD BOOKS!

In 1840, the *world's first* dental school,
The Baltimore College of Dental Surgery,
Was founded by Horace Hayden
and his exceptional student, Chapin Aaron Harris.
One year later, the BCDS conferred *the first ever*
Doctor of Dental Surgery (DDS) degree.

[N.B. Horace Hayden completed his dental preceptorship
under George Washington's dentist, John Greenwood.]

July 10

AMAZING INNOVATION!

It was not until the 1830s that Chapin Harris
Became the first dentist to insist that
all traces of caries be removed and released
From a cavity before insertion of a filling.
Can you imagine the days when a cavity, sloppily
excavated, allowed residual bacteria a continuing feast?

July 11

NOT EVEN AN "X" MARK

In Colonial days, debtors in Europe
were commonly shipped off to America
So they could work off their obligations as
"in*dentured*" servants; that's a fact.
Since most of these unfortunates
were illiterate and unable to write,
They made their *dental imprint* in wax
as a means of "sealing their contract."

July 12

FIT FOR DUTY

Civil War rifles were muzzle-loading,
and the gunpowder was wrapped in paper packets.
Union and Confederate recruiters insisted that
volunteers have at least six opposing teeth
So they could rip open the packet jackets.

[N.B.1. This is one possible origin of the term, "bite the bullet."]

[N.B.2. An alternate origin involves battlefield surgery without anesthetic; the lead was just soft enough that a soldier could bite on it without cracking his teeth.]

July 13

FOUR-F

Reluctant Civil War recruits
Couldn't escape combat with National Guard service,
So these old-time draft dodgers had all their teeth extracted;
Sitting out the conflict made them a lot less nervous!

[N.B. According to a U.S. Department of Defense report, a total of more than 550,000 soldiers died and another 400,000-plus were wounded in the U.S. Civil War.]

July 14

PET DENTITION

In the animal tooth department, cats—
Like humans—have *canines,* count 'em: four;
So why don't *dogs* have *felines*?
It's enough to make any pussycat roar!

July 15

X-RAY PIONEER

In 1896, New Orleans dentist and prolific inventor,
Dr. C. Edmund Kells, Jr.

Took the first dental x-ray of a living person in the U.S.—
exciting work for which he demonstrated great composure.

Sadly, he was unaware of the dangers
of uncontrolled radiation,

As he was in the habit of holding film in place
with his fingers during each high-dose exposure.

July 16

TERRIBLE SACRIFICE

Ten years later at age 50, after repeated radiological filming,
Kells learned that his right hand had developed cancer.

Over the next 20 years,
he submitted to the progressive amputation

Of his fingers, hand, arm, and shoulder;
then, as now, for this disease there was no answer.

[N.B. On May 7, 1928, at the age of 72, and in the grip of
intolerable pain from cancer, Dr. Kells took his own life.]

July 17

POSTHUMOUS RECOGNITION

Today, at the Louisiana State University School of Dentistry,

The C. Edmund Kells Honor Society
perpetuates Kells's memory

By annually recognizing dental students who have

Distinguished themselves both academically and clinically.

July 18

ONE-SIDED OBSERVATION

If you're right handed, you're most likely
to chew your food on the right side,

And *vice versa* for lefties.

But what if you're *ambidextrous?*

That's a question for intellectual hefties!

July 19

SMART MOUTH!

Wisdom teeth, if they emerge at all,
erupt in adults between 18 and 20.

These "third molars" have earned their popular name

Because we assume (*hope,* actually) that
mere survival of adolescence instills common sense.

Will somebody please explain that
to the rate-makers in the auto insurance game?

July 20

FIRST SCHOOL'S FIRST GRAD

The first dental school in America (and the world)

Was the Baltimore College of Dental Surgery.

The school's first graduate, Robert Arthur,

Received his diploma in 1841,
and *that* made dental history!

ROBERT TANNER FREEMAN (C. 1846-1879)

July 21

FREE MAN

The son of former slaves from North Carolina,
This history maker was born in Washington, DC.
In 1869, Robert Tanner Freeman
became one of only six members
Of the Harvard inaugural graduating class in dentistry.

July 22

IMPRESSIVE GENES

Freeman was the first African American *doctor*

Educated, degreed, and licensed in the United States—
real integration had begun.

While biographical details on the man are scarce,
we do know this:

Freeman's *grandson*, Dr. Robert C. Weaver, became
the first African American to serve in the cabinet,
Secretary of Housing and Urban Development,
of an American president—Lyndon B. Johnson.

[N.B. It should come as no surprise that before being accepted at Harvard, Robert Tanner Freeman was refused admission at two other dental schools solely because of his race.]

July 23

FIRST MAJOR DENTAL SUPPLY HOUSE

In 1825, dentist Samuel Stockton White
began commercial production

Of porcelain teeth in Philadelphia, PA.

Soon, his S.S. White Dental Manufacturing Company

Expanded to multiple locations—
even Staten Island, New York—yes, *that* far away.

July 24

SHREWD MARKETER

White's firm produced a multitude
of other products for the profession
Including electric dental drills and hydraulic dental chairs.

As a service to customers, White also published
Dental Cosmos, leading journal of the day,
Providing him with a *magnificent* medium
in which to publicize his wares.

[N.B. White's efforts established the American
dental supply market which his company
dominated throughout the 19th Century.]

July 25

TRIVIA BUFFS, LISTEN UP

White's grandson, Samuel Stockton White III,
was a gymnast and award-winning body builder.
In 1901, while visiting Paris—a *fantastic* place to eat,
The Princeton- and Cambridge University-educated
young man was introduced to world-famous sculptor,
Rodin of "The Thinker" fame,
For whom he modeled "The Athlete."

July 26

FATHER OF THE MICROSCOPE

In 1683, Antonius von Leeuwenhoek,
a Dutch tradesman,
Invented the microscope, and the news spread
'round the globe.
In the "white matter" from between his teeth (plaque),
He discovered millions of tiny "animalicules"
we now call *microbes.*

July 27

TRENCH MOUTH

The oral hygiene of Allied troops
during WWI was so lax,
And battle conditions on the front lines so dire,
That many soldiers developed ulcers
on their gums and between their teeth,
Making them unfit for service under fire.

July 28

NEVER AGAIN

The disease was labeled "trench mouth,"
And elimination of this
thoroughly-preventable affliction
Was ruled a top priority by military analysts
In any future armed confliction.

July 29

POSTWAR HYGIENE EXPLOSION

In 1824, a dentist named Peabody
Added soap to his toothpaste formulation.
A little over a century later,
our troops came home from WWII
Bringing new oral hygiene habits
to a previously carious nation.

July 30

THAT CHANGED EVERYTHING

The returning GIs created
a *huge* new oral care market
Now served by two of the largest
soap manufacturers in the land.
Colgate (Palmolive) and Proctor & Gamble (Tide),
Respectively, created today's
Total and Crest toothpaste brands.

July 31

HOW BIG *IS* IT?

In a 2004 special report, the scientifically-
estimated U.S. market for oral care products,
According to research firm Packaged Facts,
Was 7.4 *billion* dollars;
That's a *gigantic* incentive for giving caries the axe!

AUGUST

August 1

THE FIRST HYGIENISTS?

Think brushing your teeth is a chore?
And flossing is a pain in the neck?
Apparently, so did the patricians of ancient Rome;
They employed special slaves to do the job
and keep their teeth from becoming a wreck!

August 2

TRUE GRIT

In most primitive cultures, flour from a variety of grains
Was hand-milled—stone ground.
This added powdered rock to the flour
and wore bread-eater's teeth down to stubs.
In examining the skulls of those eras,
that's precisely what archeologists have found.

August 3

ACHTUNG!

"Brush and floss" is the never ending dental refrain.
Who on earth triggered this nonstop campaign?
Blame it on an American dentist in Germany—
Willoughby Dayton Miller, by name,
Who was studying the microbial basis of dental decay—
a subject considered, at the time, most arcane.

August 4

MAY I HAVE YOUR AUTOGRAPH, PLEASE

Excited about his discoveries,
Miller spread the word far and wide.
His 1890 book, *Micro-Organisms of the Human Mouth*,
attracted publicity's glare
And made his tome an instant dental bestseller
Triggering *a worldwide movement*
encouraging oral homecare.

August 5

RECOGNITION OVERDUE

So there you have it, friends;

In *my* book, Miller should've gotten the Nobel Prize—
real wealth!

Thanks to Willoughby, for the first time in history,

Individuals learned that they themselves
held the key to their own dental health.

[N.B. The very first Nobel Prize—it was
in chemistry—was awarded in 1901 to
Jacobus Henricus van 't Hoff of the Netherlands.]

August 6

INDUSTRY ROCKET BOOST

When Miller's book was first published,

Oral homecare was a fledgling market
in need of nourishing.

With the subsequent, dentist-driven,
prevention emphasis,

The toothpaste, toothbrush, mouthwash,
and floss industry started flourishing!

August 7

SPOILS-OF-WAR

Wellington defeated Napoleon on the battlefield;

Tens-of-thousands died in the misadventure.

The ensuing harvest of teeth from the dead

Led to production of the "Waterloo Denture."

August 8

WHO'S COUNTING?

Children have 20 *first, primary, baby, deciduous,* or *milk* teeth
While adults, when you include wisdom teeth, have 32.
The influential Greek philosopher, Aristotle,
(who *should* have known better),
Insisted that *men* had more teeth than *women* do.

[N.B. Adult teeth are called *succedaneous* teeth.]

August 9

IGNORANT TIMES

In the superstitious Dark Ages (about 500-1000 AD)
Folks believed an infant's teeth—
through maternal devotion—
Were produced by mother's milk,
Hence the term "milk teeth," a quaint notion.

August 10

TOO DARK

If an infant was born with a set of teeth fully erupted,
Folks believed the child was Devil-nursed—
in utero, that's where.
The fate of these "Demon offspring"?
Well, you don't want to *think* about it; don't *go* there!

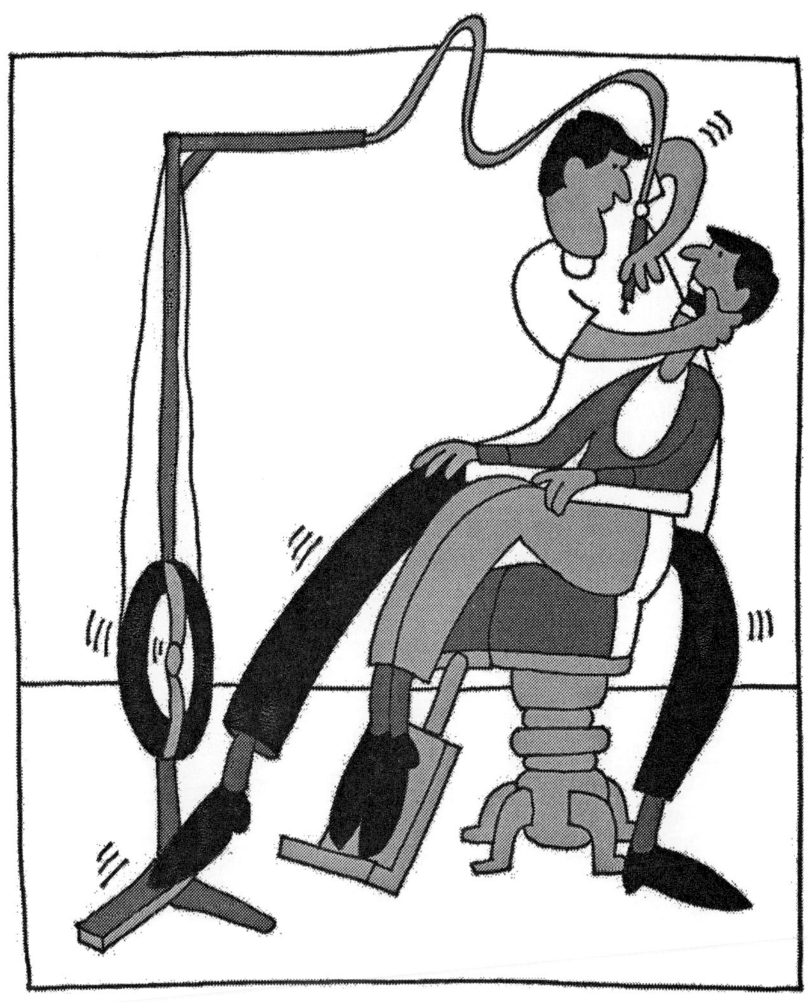

August 11

CONTORTIONIST

Now picture *this* amusing scene:
The pre-electrification era dentist
working on a patient's mouth with two hands.
With one foot pumping the treadle,
That leaves a *single foot* on which he can stand!

August 12

DENTIFRICE

Any powder or paste used to clean the teeth
is known as a "dentifrice."

This stuff, in various forms, has been around for millennia.

Contents of the earliest powders included harsh,
enamel-destructive abrasives such as talc; pulverized
alabaster, brick, coral, and oyster shells; oxen hoof ash;
iron rust; and even *pumice* (volcanic lava powder)

Plus dried flowers, ground herbs, and spices to add flava.

August 13

THEY PUT *THAT* IN THEIR MOUTHS?

The early pastes were usually concocted of powders
[see August 12]

Suspended in fluids like honey and olive oil

Plus corrosive, tooth-whitening acids and other icky stuff,

Such as urine and lizard livers (Yes!)...
enough to make anyone recoil.

August 14

First Greek "Toothbrush"

In the fifth and fourth centuries BC,
Hippocrates, the Father of Western Medicine
(of Hippocratic Oath fame) records that
The Greeks "brushed" their teeth with their fingers
Using the aforementioned "toothpaste" before they spat.

August 15

For More Than Blackboards!

During the 1800s, most dentists
concocted their own dentifrices
Which they dispensed to each patient in
a bottle, envelope, or porcelain crock.
In 1850, John M. Harris, MD, an Ohio physician with
a big interest in dentistry, kicked things up a notch:
To the formulary he added *chalk!*

August 16

IN EVERY HOME

The year 1873 was the dawn of a new era:
For the first time ever,
toothpaste-in-a-jar was *mass-produced*
And mass-marketed; *Colgate* owns this claim to fame.
You better believe it;
their innovation gave oral hygiene a *major* boost!

August 17

CRÈME DE LA CRÈME

In 1892, Connecticut dentist
Washington Wentworth Sheffield,
Creator of "Dr. Sheffield's Crème Dentifrice,"
an item most popular,
Arranged the manufacture of his toothpaste
into a collapsible tube—
An idea so bright, it was positively *solar*!

August 18

FREE TRADE ZONE

Sheffield's toothpaste packaging was an instant success;
A fact not lost on the competition.
In 1896, Colgate Dental Cream
was also offered in collapsible tubes;
Becoming Number One in serving America's
oral health was Colgate's primary mission.

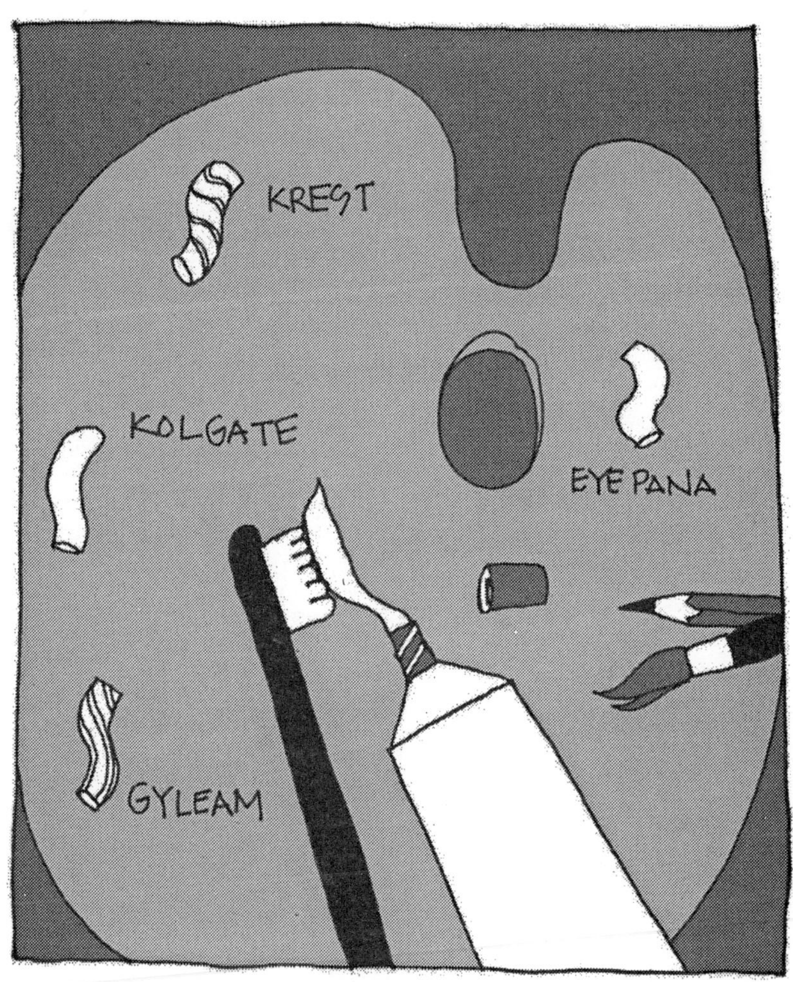

August 19

FROM PAINT TO TOOTHPASTE

We stand on the shoulders of those who have gone before.
Sheffield did *not* invent the collapsible metal tube—
don't faint;
Back in 1841, American artist John Rand patented it.
The *first* use was for—you guessed it!—*artists' paint.*

August 20

THE FIRST DENTAL ASSISTANT

In 1885, busy New Orleans dentist C. Edmund Kells, Jr.

Hired a young woman to replace
a departing male employee.

Two years later, he wrote "Methods and Means,"
a paper published in the *Ohio Journal of Dental Science,*

In which he made reference to the benefits
of engaging a *woman* in this capacity.

[N.B. This is the same Dr. Kells who, eleven years
later, would achieve fame as the world's
pioneer in the use of dental x-rays.]

August 21

SENSE AND SENSIBILITY

While the acceptance of female assistants was slow

In the male-dominated profession,

By the turn-of-the-century, it was not unusual
to see *this* sign in a dental office window:

"Lady in Attendance," reflecting within the practice
a keen Victorian-era discretion.

August 22

INDISPENSABLE

In 1911, New York City dentist Dr. Henry Fowler

Hired Juliette A. Southard as his full-time assistant

And quickly discovered the value
of her considerable administrative talent.

Ten years later, in a conference technical paper, the good
doctor gave a strong recommendation to his colleagues:
that to hiring dental assistants they should not be resistant.

[N.B. The duties of today's dental assistant may
include instrument cleaning, chairside assistance,
inventory management, scheduling patient
appointments, bookkeeping, and reception.]

August 23

BEGINNINGS

In 1917, America's first dental assistant society
was founded in Nebraska.

Four years later, Southard formed
a New York City sister organization.

Soon afterward, she teamed up with the presidents
of the Chicago and Cook County
Dental Assistants Associations,
and together they successfully petitioned

The ADA for permission to attend its 1923 convention
in Cleveland, Ohio, giving them real cause for celebration!

August 24

HAIL TO THE CHIEF!

One year later—at a Dallas meeting in 1924,
A constitution and bylaws were adopted
and officers elected who collectively gave birth to the
American Dental Assistants Association,
quite an achievement.

In 1925, lawyers were paid, papers were filed,
and the ADAA officially became an Illinois corporation.

By acclamation, the officers elected
Juliette Southard as its their president!

August 25

FAMILY CONNECTION

Bridgeport, Connecticut, dentist Alfred Fones
Had a cousin, Irene Newman, who was smart to the core.
'Tho he hired her as an office assistant
He soon discovered she could handle a whole lot more.

August 26

AMERICA'S FIRST DENTAL HYGIENIST

In 1905, Fones and Newman made history
When he taught her to clean children's teeth
By removing plaque and tartar
which she found in abundance
Circling each little tooth like a wreath.

August 27

PILOT PROGRAM

While Ms. Newman taught the children
how to keep their pearlies looking white,
Dr. Fones scheduled the youngsters for periodic
appointments—what we now call *recall!*
Soon the drop in kiddie caries was self-evident
So the good Doc set about making dental prophylaxis
available to Bridgeport schoolchildren, one and all.

August 28

ANOTHER AMERICAN FIRST

In 1913, having demonstrated the effectiveness
of his caries-prevention programs,

Dr. Fones established a formal,
two-year school for dental hygienists.

While a garage behind his
carriage-house office was the venue

Don't let the modesty of the facility fool you.

August 29

FAT CHANCE

Picture this: It's 1913,

For still-disenfranchised females,
the right to *!vote!* is out of the question;

Yet some crazy Connecticut dentist
wants to set up a *school*

To teach WOMEN a brand-new dental profession!

August 30

TOP GUN EDUCATORS

Who on earth would be willing
to teach hygiene in a lowly *garage*?

Wellllllll, how about the *deans* of the Harvard and
the University of Pennsylvania dental school,

Seven professors from Yale and two from Columbia,
plus a *Who's Who* of the world's leading practitioners;

That was the faculty pool!

August 31

FRONT LINE SOLDIERS IN THE WAR ON CARIES

In 1915, the inaugural class of the
Fones School of Dental Hygiene

Produced 27 history-making graduates—
an event without precedent!

Many found immediate employment
in the Bridgeport school district

Where they reduced childhood dental caries
by a whopping 75 percent!

[N.B. Today, the Fones School of Dental Hygiene
is part of the University of Bridgeport; there are more
than 200 dental hygiene schools in the U.S.; and the
nation is served by 120,000 registered dental hygienists.]

SEPTEMBER

September 1

AQUATIC FOWL AND DENTAL INSTRUMENT

Consider the pelican:
Its beak can hold more than its belly can.
Pelican is also the name of a 19th-century "pliers"
Created expressly to extract teeth from woman or man.

September 2

LOCKSMITH-INSPIRED

In the evolution of dental extraction technology
The pelican—so named because it resembled the bird—
was followed by the tooth key.
Crafted by locksmiths,
The tee-handled device was placed over the tooth and
twisted back and forth until the roots were *freeeeeeeeee!*

September 3

PRIVATE PRIVACY

Early in the Civil War, Union Army dental extractions
Were performed in the quiet interior of many a medical tent.
From time to time, passers-by would be shaken
As ear-splitting howls, from behind canvas, the air did rent.

September 4

ALFRESCO DENTISTRY

After a while, the scenario was altered;
Extractions were conducted *outdoors*—
in the presence of many an animal and bird.
Audiences of 100-or-more soldiers were invited—
From that time on, not a macho patient murmur was heard.

September 5

STAG'S LEAP

British Columbia's Francis Wharton liked to hunt;
And some years ago, brought down a nice-sized deer.
With visions of venison steak leaping in his brain,
His shortage of teeth brought Francis more than one tear.

September 6

WHAT TO DO?

Wharton pulled the teeth from his prize,
Ground them down to a serviceable size,
And, using Plastic Wood from a shelf in his shed,
Fitted dentures to the gums in his head.

September 7

BUCK TEETH

The deer's choppers were soon secured to the base
Making use of common household cement;
And Wharton *thrilled* to his venison feast,
A long-missed gustatory event.

[N.B. This incredible story, verified by the British Columbia Wildlife Agency, is adapted from *Foley's Footnotes: A Treasury of Dentistry* by noted dental historian, Gardner P.H. Foley.]

September 8

OLD TESTAMENTARY EXPRESSION

In Job 18:19, we learn

That the author of the story,
reduced to flesh and bone,

Has escaped the hand of God
with naught but the "skin of his teeth";

His *gums* were the only flesh he had left;
listen careful' now; you may *still* hear Job moan!

September 9

ATHENIAN DOC

Greek physician Hippocrates,

Who lived about the 5th Century BC,

Founded the first medical school

And taught lots of stuff—including *dentistry!*

[N.B. Hippocrates said: "The physician should know what the physician before him has known if he does not want to defraud himself and others."]

September 10

32 TEETH; 32 PARAGRAPHS!

To share his medical knowledge,
Hippocrates also wrote books—

Still available for study today.

He devoted 32 paragraphs in his works

On how to treat teeth and keep cavities away.

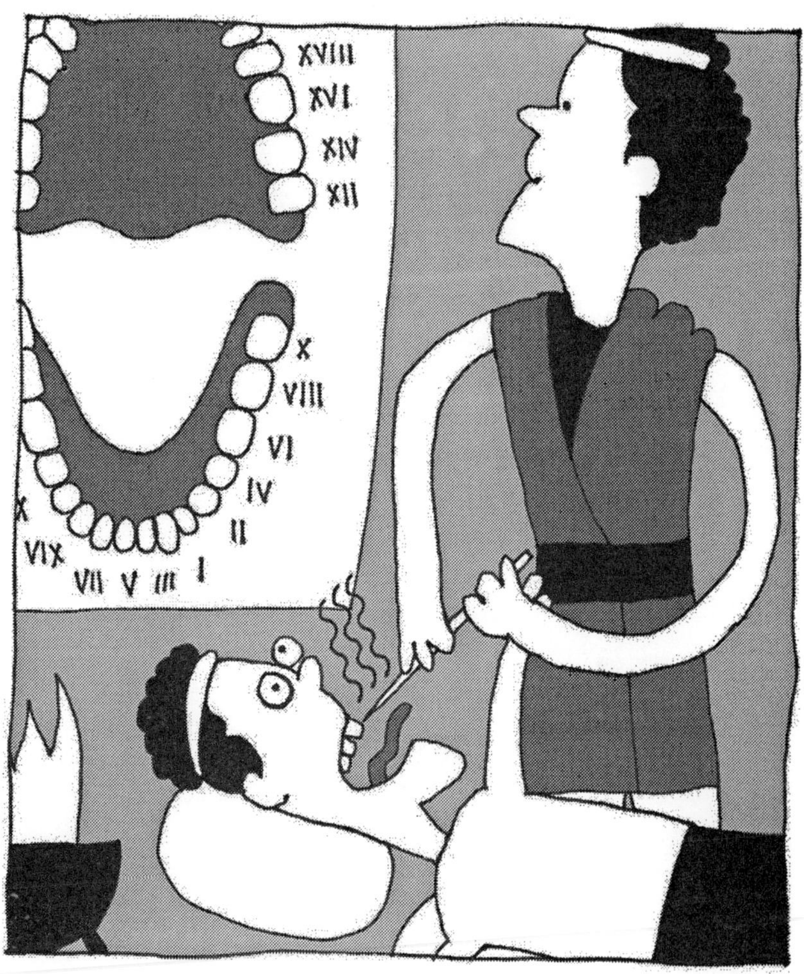

September 11

HOTTER THAN *JALAPEÑOS!*

Hippocrates' early contributions to dentistry
Included assigning each tooth a unique number... creativity you *must* admire!
And prescribing *this* delicate treatment for deep rot:
Cauterize the cavity with a long, *red-hot wire!*

September 12

SPAGHETTI WASN'T *ALL* HE DISCOVERED!

The Chinese have been manufacturing porcelain
For more than 4,000 years.

In the late 13th Century, Marco Polo was the first
European to observe this translucent ceramic

And bring back samples to the nobles of Europe
for which he received *lots* of money and loud cheers!

[N.B. Porcelain was named by Marco Polo
after a translucent *pork* (porcine)
delicacy favored by the Romans.]

September 13

FOUR CENTURY QUEST

Europeans unsuccessfully attempted
to duplicate the Chinese product

For more than 400 years

Until around 1765 when the secret ingredient,
kaolin, was discovered in abundance and mined

In Saint-Yrieix-la-Perche, France, where they celebrated
the occasion with *Champagne*, not with beers!

[N.B. Kaolin, a very fine, white clay, is not only used
in porcelain; it is also used in *medicine*, especially
as an adsorbent in the treatment of diarrhea.
Ever hear of *Kao*pectate?]

September 14

INTELLECTUAL PROPERTY CLAIM

Soon afterward, the world was introduced to
a new French export: Limoges porcelain,

Regarded today as simply the finest.

With the newly-available material, Parisian dentist,
Nicolas Dubois de Chémant,

Invented the world's first porcelain *teeth* which he
patented in 1789 and then probably celebrated
in the usual French way—with a winefest.

[N.B. When individual porcelain teeth were first
introduced in America, Francophobic dentists
referred to the prosthetics as "French beans."]

September 15

MILITARY POETRY (NOT AN OXYMORON)

"When time has stripped our armoury bare,

Dubois steps in with subtle heed;

New grinders and new cutters gives;
With his we laugh, with his we feed.

Long live Chémant, friend in need."

[N.B. Written by 80 year-old General
Comte de Martagne, an obviously-grateful,
full-denture patient of de Chémant.]

September 16

PRECIOUS STONES

Mick Jagger is a flamboyant showman;
He's always been *waaaaaaaaaay* too cool!
A generation ago, he put an emerald on his incisor,
Later replacing it with a *diamond* tooth-jewel.

[N.B. For more about tooth art, see October 1 below.]

September 17

MESMERIZING POTENTIAL!

Pain has been with us since Man
First stubbed his bare big toe.
Hypnotism, in one form or another,
has been around for millennia;
Is it possible that this "trance"
could relieve our pain-related woe?

September 18

THE FATHER OF HYPNOTISM

Scottish-born, Edinburgh-trained, physician
James Braid studied the phenomenon,

Testing it progressively on his wife,
a servant, and then a friend.

In 1842, he coined the words,
hypnotism, hypnotize, and *hypnotist,*

In *The Rationale of Nervous Sleep*, a landmark
book of research findings that he penned.

[N.B. Hypnosis is named after
the Greek god of sleep, Hypnos.]

September 19

IN A CITY NEAR YOU!

Hypnodontics is the practice
of dentistry using hypnotism

To deal with pain and deep anxiety
as well as control extreme gag reflex.

Today it is the subject of serious research
at several major universities,

And dental practitioners employing the regimen
may be found in *every* metroplex.

September 20

I ♥ My Teeth

The Chinese economy is looking up.

So people, they're eating more sweets;
offered candy, they cannot say "Nay!"

The result: A cavity *epidemic* among
China's 1.2 *billion* citizens.

In 1989, the government acted to stem the tide
declaring September 20 "Love Teeth Day."

September 21

CLEVER!

15th-century Chinese made
bamboo-handled toothbrushes;
For bristles, they used the stiff neck hairs
of Siberian wild boars.
[You obviously had to be *rich* to afford one of those!]
Today's *nylon* toothbrushes, introduced in 1937,
aren't nearly as coarse.

September 22

STRING THEORY

The ancients cleaned 'tween their teeth
With imported Chinese silk thread,
While modern folks keep cavities away
With nylon floss instead.

September 23

THE FATHER OF MODERN DENTAL IMPLANTS

In 1952, a Swedish orthopedic surgeon
named Per-Ingvar Brånemark,

Working at a modest laboratory
in the university town of Lund,

Inserted small titanium chambers into the legs of *rabbits*

To microscopically study bone marrow activity,
and got *stunned*!

September 24

WHAT A NUISANCE!

A few months later, when Brånemark tried to *extract*

The bone-anchored titanium,

He found it impossible to do so—the bone had grown
into every microscopic nook and cranny of the chambers.

Not fully appreciating the significance of his discovery,
he just tucked it away in his cranium.

September 25

TEST, STUDY, TEST, STUDY!

Eight years later, Brånemark
was continuing his research

At Sweden's Gothenburg University.

By this time, his subjects had advanced to the
canine species [Don't dogs *chase* rabbits?],

And *dental* implantation would
soon become a reality!

September 26

NAMING THE PHENOMENON

Don't know why it is,

But medicine would be *impossible* without
exotic names from the Latin nation.

"Os" is Latin for *bone*, while "integration"...
well, you know what *that* is!

So Brånemark labeled the phenomenon
he discovered "osseointegration."

September 27

TOP OF THE EVOLUTION LADDER!

Dr. Brånemark's first titanium dental implant
was on a beagle—quite successful.

With that progress, in 1965 the doctor advanced to
his first *human* patient in pursuit of his obsession;

That gentleman was 34 year-old Gösta Larsson,
who received four implants in his lower jaw.

It's now been 40 years, and Mr. Larsson's smile
is *still* making a lasting impression!

[N.B. According to the Academy of Osseointegration, more than a half-million implants are now being placed surgically worldwide *each year*.]

September 28

AN ORGANIZATION OF THEIR OWN

The American Dental Association

Recognizes several dental specialties:
Currently there are nine.

For the all-important *general* dentist,

The Academy of General Dentistry works just fine.

[N.B. Each dental specialty has its own national organization. In 1952, Dr. Thaddeus V. Weclew founded, and served as first president of, the AGD. Today's 35,000 AGD members are required to complete a minimum of 75 hours of continuing education every three years.]

September 29

SETTING TEETH ON EDGE

HOTSPUR: "Marry,
And I am glad of it with all my heart:
I had rather be a kitten and cry mew
Than one of these same metre ballad-mongers;
I had rather hear a brazen canstick turn'd,
Or a dry wheel grate on the axle-tree;
And that would set my *teeth* nothing *on edge*,
Nothing so much as mincing poetry:
'Tis like the forced gait of a shuffling nag."

[N.B. Excerpted from Shakespeare's *Henry IV.*]

September 30

MARK TWAIN ADAPTATION

"Age enlarges and enriches
The powers of some musical instruments—
Notably those of the violin—
But it seems to set a piano's *teeth on edge.*"

[N.B. Excerpted from Samuel Clemens's story, *Some Rambling Notes of an Idle Excursion.*]

OCTOBER

October 1

PRECIOUS SMILES

Evidence shows that around 900 AD,
the Mayans used bow drills

To make holes in front teeth so that onlays

Of jade, turquoise, and
other colorful stones could be applied.

Ya gotta admit, it's got a certain *cachet*!

October 2

OCEAN BIOLOGY

Coral reefs "grow" from a buildup of calcium carbonate.

Tartar is the same thing—a buildup of calcium carbonate!

Sooooo, if you don't control plaque with good oral hygiene

A coral reef will flourish in your mouth,
feasting on what you recently ate!

[N.B. Any seasoned hygienist will tell you about the patient whose teeth were so encrusted with tartar there was no space between them. Talk about *disgusting*!]

October 3

PERIO PRIMER

Here's how it works:

Your teeth stick out of your jaw, Jack.

Your healthy, pink gums seal the tooth-jaw interface
like a snug turtleneck around your own neck,

Shielding the tooth roots and jawbone from plaque.

October 4

SEEING RED

When you neglect your hygiene,

The plaque- and tartar-causing
bacteria go to work on your gums

(After all, gum tissue is softer than
tooth roots or jawbone, got it?)

In no time at all, you've got *gingivitis*,
your gums are bleeding, and you feel really glumz!

October 5

PATH TO PAIN

Once the gums start to erode,

Tartar has a clear shot;
on your jaw it will soon be noshin'.

And since a healthy jaw is what
anchors the roots of your teeth;

When jawbone erodes, choppers loosen—you can even
wiggle 'em, and it's abscess time; we're not joshin'.

October 6

TAILOR TALK

When the gums pull away from your teeth,
The result is plaque-friendly pockets.
Bacteria critters like to call these home
And dump poop in your alveolar sockets.

October 7

FINANCIAL CONSIDERATIONS

"Deep Pockets" usually means "access to lots of money."
When tartar hardens in the deep pockets of your gums,
The tissue can no longer stick to your teeth.
That's when we elect root-planing;
treatmentwise, it can amount to large sums.

October 8

NIGHTMARES

After years of neglect, things can get nasty,
And the hygienically-lazy will experience all the delights
Of jawbone and gum grafts
plus other gruesome procedures.
Worrying about that is guaranteed
to keep *anybody* up nights!

October 9

ROAD TO RECOVERY

Periodontic treatment is *waaaaay*
better than no teeth at all.
For a referral, consult your dentist—
all year long through the end of December,
Or visit the website of the
American Academy of Periodontology;
They'll gladly help you connect
with a specially-trained member.

October 10

AHHHHHHH, THE 1800S

A couple of centuries ago, dental offices
were commonly located in the *homes* of practitioners;
Neither electricity nor plumbing
graced these pre-Victorian, front-room parlors.
Here, dentists excavated cavities by
foot-pumping their treadle-drills
And patients attempted modesty and decorum
while spitting into cuspidors.

October 11

Let the Sun Shine In

In the absence of electricity, *nature* provided
The brightest available light in the living-room operatory
So dental chairs were placed before the front window;
Patients' lack of privacy is the sad part of this story.

October 12

THE DREAM

Schoolteacher Lucy Beaman Hobbs (1833-1910)
had an unwavering ambition:

She wanted to be a *doctor*;
she had the guts and intellect to be a real contender.

In 1859, Hobbs applied
to Cincinnati's Eclectic College of Medicine

Where she was *rejected*—solely because of her gender.

October 13

FIRST TUTOR

Lucy then began private study
under a member of CECM's faculty.

He, recognizing her single-minded devotion
and the obstacles that lay ahead,

Gave the matter serious thought before recommending

That she pursue a *dental* career instead.

October 14

UNSTOPPABLE MINDSET!

Next, Hobbs studied privately
Under the Ohio College of Dental Surgery's *dean,*
And then apprenticed herself
to a practicing graduate of that same school.
Lucy obviously had a plan;
and her enthusiasm was *unquenchably* keen!

[N.B. For the identity of the mystery dean, go to November 2 and all will be revealed.]

October 15

REJECTED—AGAIN!

When she applied for admission to OCDS in 1861
And was rejected because she wasn't a man—
too *frail,* was their excuse, still the wrong gender,
The determined Lucy
opened her own practice in Cincinnati;
She absolutely *refused* to surrender!

[N.B. At that time in Ohio, licensing requirements had not yet been enacted for the dental profession. Quite literally, *anyone* could hang out a shingle!]

October 16

GO WEST!

In 1862, Hobbs moved to Iowa,
where she practiced for three years.
In 1865, she was elected to membership
In the newly-formed Iowa State Dental Society
And sent as a *delegate* to the ADA convention
in Chicago—that was quite a trip!

October 17

HAIL THE GRADUATE!

In November of 1865, Hobbs was finally admitted
To the Ohio College of Dental Surgery *senior class*,
And on her graduation in 1866—*a mere four months later*,
Dr. Lucy Beaman Hobbs became the first woman in the world
to receive a dental degree; with flying colors, she did pass!

October 18

THE REST OF THE STORY

A year later, our heroine married a gentleman
named James M. Taylor.
Soon the couple moved to Lawrence, Kansas, where
Lucy taught her *spouse* to be a dentist—*there's* a switch!
At the time of her retirement 19 years later (hubby died),
they had built a flourishing practice, that remarkable pair!

[N.B. Today, approximately half of the students
entering dental schools are women.]

October 19

South of the Border

In Mexico, the Tooth Fairy's counterpart is
The Tooth Mouse
Like the TF, this cute little rodent
exchanges teeth for treasures.
Since mice are nocturnal critters,
that's when they have the run of the house.

October 20

THE GOODYEAR VULCANITE DENTURE SAGA

It's important to note at the outset
that the featured players in our story—

The pioneering inventors of rubber goods
in the Goodyear family—

Had *nothing whatsoever* to do with the founding

Of the Goodyear Tire and Rubber Company!

[N.B. The name of the Akron, Ohio-based tire-manufacturing firm, started in 1898 by Frank Seiberling, was chosen in homage to Charles Goodyear (1800-1860) and to associate the new enterprise with the origins of the rubber industry.]

October 21

HUNDRED YEAR-OLD LABORATORY CURIOSITY

In 1844, dedicated inventor/inept businessman,
Charles Goodyear,

Secured the first U.S. patent for vulcanized rubber.

Before Charles did his thing,
hot rubber was soft, runny and gooey

While *cold* rubber—hard, cracked easily—wasn't limber.

[N.B. The first use for natural latex (India rubber) was as an eraser to "rub out" pencil marks, hence the name, "rubber."]

October 22

VULCAN: ROMAN GOD OF FIRE

What Charles discovered after
mucho bucks, sweat and years
Involved the application of heat
To a pot of latex and sulfur—
Apparently a difficult scientific feat.

[N.B. Charles Goodyear consistently plowed back into his research every dime he made and was in and out of debtor's prison all of his adult life. At the time of his death in 1860, he owed almost $200,000—millions in today's dollars!]

October 23

OUT OF NOWHERE—AND BACK

In 1864, an unknown Boston dentist,
John A. Cummings,
After 12 years of rejections, secured an
"application patent" on dentures—*Wheeeee!*—
Made with the Goodyear Vulcanization process
That he soon transferred to the
Goodyear Dental Vulcanite Company.

October 24

INSIDER DEALING

Josiah Bacon, treasurer of the
Goodyear Dental Vulcanite Company,
Then *personally* secured all of
Cummings's patent right
And, from that time forward,
Pursued licensing fees from
America's dentists with all his might.

October 25

PORK BELLY MONOPOLY

Bacon soon had infringement suits
going from coast to coast,
And legions of dentists responded by forming
The American Dental Protective Society
But were no match for Bacon's attorneys,
who were swarming.

October 26

UNRELENTING PURSUIT

After the Supreme Court ruled favorably
in 1880 on Bacon's patent infringement appeal,

He pledged to make an example of
Dr. Samuel P. Chalfant—the most defiant.

He chased the good dentist from Wilmington,
Delaware to St. Louis and on to San Francisco;

Bacon wanted Chalfant's defeat
to be *huge*, to be *giant!*

October 27

SUNRISE SERVICE

The Judge-by-the-Bay found Chalfant guilty

And ordered him big money to pay.

So Chalfant made restitution—with a bullet—

Delivered to Bacon's belly early the next morn
at the posh Baldwin Hotel on Easter Sunday.

October 28

LIGHT SENTENCE

Chalfant was defended by
San Francisco's preeminent Hall McAllister,

But the jury found our doc *guilty*
of murder in the second-degree.

At San Quentin, he served five years
(outside the walls) as prison dentist before

Being released for good behavior;
nevermore did he flee.

October 29

FIZZLE AND DIE

At the time of Bacon's death

Only two years remained
on the Vulcanite denture claim.

The company ceased enforcement efforts
and did not attempt extension

Since no surviving corporate officer
would risk another dentist's aim.

October 30

The Hinman

Considered the first dental clinic

For serious-minded continuing education,

The 1911 Atlanta Midwinter Clinic

Established professional meeting standards for the rest of the nation.

[N.B. The non-profit clinic was later renamed the Thomas P. Hinman Dental Meeting after its founder. In March 2005, more than 23,000 dental professionals participated in the 93rd Annual Session at the Georgia World Congress Center.]

October 31

Spooky Aftermath

All children love Halloween candy,

But teeth and stuff that's sticky-sweet

Make for a carious combination;

So avoid caramels *especially* for a smile that's not a trick; it's a treat!

NOVEMBER

November 1

CAN'T RUN A DENTAL PRACTICE WITHOUT 'EM

On November 16, 1864, Patent Number 263,
The Confederate Patent Office did provide
To Thomas B. Taylor of Montgomery, Alabama,
On a "machine for making cotton rolls"; an
invention worthy of down-home Southern pride.

November 2

MYSTERY MAN

Now, let's revisit America's first woman dental-school graduate, Lucy Hobbs, and ask this burning question:

"Who was that OCDS *dean* who tutored the woman and then rejected her application?"

It was Jonathan Taft, DDS, childhood classmate of the future General Ulysses T. Grant, that's who.

Some even assert he was related to the future presidential Taft family—an important connection in this great nation!

[N.B. See October 12 for the Lucy Hobbs story.]

November 3

MUCHO MACHO

As Dean of OCDS, Taft didn't rule like King George;

Instead, faculty consensus he attempted to forge.

When the academic wimps insisted
women were much too frail,

It was Taft who had to enforce this view—
sadly, all too male.

November 4

REDUX

And when, somewhat later, Lucy reapplied
to an OCDS whose faculty had seen the light,

It was Taft who had the honor of accepting her app.

Two years after Lucy achieved her doctoral distinction,

Taft was elected president of the American Dental
Association—that really put *him* on the map!

November 5

STAY WITH ME; WE'RE GOING SOMEWHERE WITH THIS!

In 1875, Jonathan Taft became the founding dean
of the University of Michigan School of Dentistry,

America's second (after Harvard) university-
affiliated dental school for training
soldiers in the war against tooth decay!

Taft instituted the country's first full-four-year
academic dental program—today's standard,

And, in 1886, presided over the admission of Ida Gray.

November 6

ANOTHER TAFT FEMALE FIRST

Dr. Gray, who in 1890 graduated from
the University of Michigan School of Dentistry,

Became the first African American woman—
in the world—to earn a *dental* degree.

Remarkably, it was our very same Jonathan Taft

Who helped make her academic dream a reality!

November 7

PRESS RELATIONS

After graduation, Ida returned home to Cincinnati

Where she established a very successful practice;
her life was full!

A hometown news editor was later heard to say of Dr. Gray,

"Her blushing, winning ways make you feel
like finding an extra tooth...to allow her to pull."

November 8

GREEK BRACE

If Hippocrates was the greatest
physician from ancient Greece,
"Who was second-in-line?" you may ask us.
'Tho he was also a Greek,
Claudius Galen (c. 129-c. 216 AD) chose *Rome*
as home for his medico-dental practus.

November 9

INSIDE SOURCE

"What made Claudius such hot stuff?"
You continue your interrogation;
He was the first to identify *nerves* in teeth
And suggest that pulp is where
sensation has its origination.

November 10

HOLY SMOKE!

Bruxism is an odd-sounding term;
It means "to gnash the teeth,"
and is based on the word *brychein* from the Greek.
There are numerous, hellish, Biblical references to it—
Old Testament and New—
Most often teamed with *weeping* and *wailing*, a
combination that should make *most* people freak!

[N.B. The next quatrain is an old joke I've retold
in rhyme; I hope you enjoy it as much as I did.]

November 11

HELL'S QUARTERMASTER

A sweet old lady approached her preacher
after a fire-and-brimstone sermon:
"I'm afraid I've already lost my teeth," she sighed,
"So I won't worry about gnashing them
if I don't go to heaven."
"Madam," the cleric heatedly exclaimed,
"for those in need of teeth, *they will be supplied!*"

November 12

SYMPTOMS

Bruxism *diagnosis* is the easy part;
The occlusal (bite) surfaces of your teeth
will be flatter than most.
Or your spouse may report
that your choppers squeak nocturnally
Like chalk on a blackboard—
untreated, your teeth will eventually be toast!

November 13

CHILL!

The University of Maryland Medical Center
States that one in three people suffer this condition.
The major causes are anger, frustration and stress,
So *relaxation* should be your primary mission!

November 14

TREATMENT

The most-often recommended first step
Is to have a dentist fit you with a *nightguard*.
This custom-molded plastic appliance
is worn while you nightmare or dream
And cushions your teeth when,
in REM sleep, you bite hard.

November 15

LIGHT MY FIRE

Smoking conveys a look of real sophistication.

Nicotine-yellow teeth flash a daffodil smile.

Those oral-cancer surgery scars add
real character to the face,

And that chunk of infected jawbone
will be missing for quite a while.

November 16

SEEING EYE DOC

Charles D. Kelman, MD (1930-2004),
an ophthalmic surgeon,

Developed an *outpatient* cataract operation

That's helped over 100 million souls and counting.

For each and every one,
his operation delivers visual salvation.

[N.B. As you read the following quatrains,
the dental connection will be revealed.]

November 17

FAKO WHAT?

Before Kelman, cataract removal
meant ten days in hospital,

But was radically simplified by this medical pioneer.

His phacoemulsification
procedure proved *great* for the eye,

But slipping off the tongue,
was always *murder* on the ear.

[N.B. *Phaco* is Greek for "lens" and *emulsi* is "milked out."]

November 18

FORGET THE QUARTERS

The operation uses a vibrating, ultrasonic tip
To break up the blinding cataract
Which is then suctioned away
with a very thin needle
Making the original eye intact.

November 19

DENTAL CHAIR EPIPHANY

Turns out Kelman was having his teeth
cleaned ultrasonically one day
When, the famous light bulb went off—
the *Eureka!* moment occurred.
"I could use this technique to *pulverize* cataracts,"
we assume he thought,
Because in 1967, the vision of his patients
suddenly was no longer blurred.

November 20

EXTRA INCENTIVE

Who knows, the next time you have your teeth cleaned
You too, might get a fantastic idea, file your patent claim,
And, like Kelman, win the National Medal of Technology,
the American Academy of Achievement Award,
And be inducted into the
National Inventors Hall of Fame!

November 21

THE ROMANTIC HISTORY OF RUBBER GLOVES

In the early 1890s,
famed physician Dr. William S. Halsted
Was the Johns Hopkins Hospital's top surgeon;
While Miss Caroline Hampton was head operating nurse
And the person for whom the doctor's love did burgeon.

November 22

PRE-OSHA

At the time, nurse Hampton's hands
Presented an occupational safety concern;
Immersion in antiseptic fluids:
Carbolic acid and bichloride of mercury,
were making them do a slow *burn*.

November 23

DUAL AGENDA

Halstead's distress over Hampton was bifurcated:
While he gallantly desired her personal well being,
His surgical performance was severely diminished
Without her supporting O.R. skills,
everyone was agreeing.

November 24

GOODYEAR TO THE RESCUE

In search of a solution to this daunting problem,

Halstead ultimately conceived
a brilliant remedy for his soul mate.

He contacted the Goodyear India Rubber Glove Company,
headquartered in Naugatuck, Connecticut,

And asked them, a pair of
thin rubber gloves with gauntlets, to create.

November 25

WEDDING BELLS

In no time at all, Goodyear produced gloves as requested;

And post-operative infections no longer patients infested.

The team of Halstad and Hampton
was finally back in business;

Before long, the couple wed
and in their marriage bed rested.

November 26

HYGIENIC COURTSHIP

Roses are red,

And violets are blue,

But if you don't brush and floss,

She'll never marry you!

November 27

MIRACLE ON ICE

When the 1980 American hockey team brought home the gold
Sports Illustrated said it was
"The greatest sports moment of the 20th Century."
It happened at the Winter Olympiad
in Lake Placid, New York
Where even the undefeated-for-20-years
Russians did they bury!

[N.B. Want more? Be sure to see the Walt Disney Pictures movie, *Miracle,* chronicling the 1980 U.S. hockey team and starring actor Kurt Russell, now available on DVD.]

November 28

JOURNEY TO GOLD

It was a slap shot that tied the game with Sweden
That is worthy of note for our story.
"Who was the player who *drilled* that shot," you ask?
It was twenty-two year-old Defenseman, Bill Baker,
who helped our team to glory.

November 29

MYSTERY MAN

And *who*, you may ask, *is* this Bill Baker,
and why should we even care?
Well, after a three-year post-Olympic stint in the NHL,
Our hero became a DENTIST,
an oral and maxillofacial surgeon to be precise,
Who has a four-office practice in Minnesota,
where he and his family now dwell.

[N.B. After his NHL retirement, Baker earned his dental degree in St. Louis, Missouri, before completing his oral and maxillofacial residency at the University of Minnesota, in all, a nine-year process!]

November 30

WHAT'S UP, DOC?

He's got enormous, cavity-free incisors,
That Bugs Bunny, the cartoon rabbit.
However, Mel Blanc, his onscreen voice,
Was *allergic* to the carrot habbit!

[N.B.1. A group of hares is called a "husk."]

[N.B.2. Rabbit incisors and molars grow as a rabbit ages, roughly equaling the gradual loss due to wear and tear from biting and eating.]

DECEMBER

December 1

FIREWATER

In the Old West, the most readily available,
And commonly used, dental anesthetic was whiskey.
While it's easy to understand the *patient's* interest in getting numb before an extraction,
Many a frontier dentist sought "whiskey courage" *for himself* before working on pain-stricken, gun-toting clients, a procedure obviously most risky.

December 2

TOOTHPICK CAPITAL OF THE WORLD

The Strong Wood Products plant in Strong, Maine is reportedly the biggest toothpick manufacturing plant in the United States.

Only ten humans are needed to produce an average output of 20 million toothpicks daily.

Maine produces 90% of the toothpicks made in the United States.

Warning, you wouldn't want to use these picks on your ukulele!

[N.B. Way back in 1872, Silas Noble and J.P. Cooley secured a patent on the first toothpick-manufacturing machine.]

December 3

TIME ON YOUR HANDS?

In a faraway land,
there's a *toothpick museum*—admission free;

A sixty-minute tour should do the trick
for the even most *dedicated* fan

All you have to do is get an airline ticket to:

Koeisha Ltd. near Osaka in Kawachinagano, Japan.

[N.B.1. Koeisha Ltd., manufacturer of 95% of Japan's toothpicks, is in a heavily forested area surrounded by the Katsuragi and Kongo mountains.]

[N.B.2. Kawachinagano is the "sister city" of Carmel, California!]

December 4

PHILADELPHIA TO PARIS

It was 1847 when young Thomas Wiltberger Evans
won an award

For his gold fillings at Philadelphia's Franklin Institute.

Soon after, he set up practice in the French
City of Lights

And quickly became dentist
to the famous and non-destitute.

[N.B. Evans received his dental diploma from the Jefferson Medical College in 1843 and learned his lab skills from a local gold and silver artisan. One of Evans's JMC classmates was S.S. White, founder of the nation's first dental supply company.]

December 5

FRENCH INFLUENCE

Evans was not only an extraordinary Parisian *dentiste*,

His confidential manner made him the perfect liaison

Between European heads, and near-heads, of state

Including Louis-Napoleon,
The "Little Corporal's" sister's son.

December 6

FRENCH GOLD

Evans made it a practice in his practice
Not to charge fees to his wealthy clients—an unusual trait
So they compensated him with insider tips
Making the dentist a multi-millionaire in Paris real estate!

December 7

ROYAL COUP

In 1852, Louis-Napoleon Bonaparte
Instituted a parliamentary coup d'état
And made Dr. Evans "Surgeon Dentist"
to the imperial court
Of Napoleon III, Emperor of France—imagine that!

December 8

TRANS-ATLANTIC MISSION

Events in America prior to the Civil War

Were of great interest to
European tobacco- and cotton-lovers,

So Evans was dispatched by Napoleon
on a fact-finding trip in 1864;

That's when the dentist met Lincoln, Seward,
and Grant to see what he could uncoverz.

December 9

HISTORIC INFLUENCE

It was Evans's report to Napoleon,
Predicting a quick Union victory in the war,
That stopped France (and other European nations)
From aiding the Confederacy and a whole lot more.

December 10

ROYAL RESCUE

When N-III fell out of favor with the common folk,

The rabble called for the head of their
Spanish-born empress-queen.

Who whisked the beautiful lady off to England?

It was that Evans fellow who helped her quit
French cuisine and avoid the guillotine.

[N.B. *The Dentist and the Empress: The Adventures of Dr. Tom Evans in Gas-lit Paris* by Gerald Carson makes a great read for those who've enjoyed *The Scarlet Pimpernel.*]

December 11

DENTAL PHILANTHROPIST

In 1897, Evans and his wife
died eleven months apart in Philadelphia.

The major portion of their considerable fortune,

Including income from real estate investments
in Pennsylvania and New York,

Was left to the Dental School of
the University of Pennsylvania.

December 12

DOUBLE TOOTHACHES

One goose, two geese; one moose, two *meese*?

One tooth, two teeth; one booth, two *beeth*?

The more I think about it, the more I realize:

The English language hurts my teeth!

December 13

MONA LISA SMILE

Professor Donald Sassoon of Britain's London University,
Is the author of *Mona Lisa: The History of the World's Most Famous Painting*—a real book gem.
When an interviewer asked why Mona Lisa's smile doesn't display her teeth, he offered this observation:
"In the 15th Century, teeth were *terrible*, so they're not going to show them."

December 14

ADORING WIFE

I love my handsome hubby,
To me, he's Mr. Right;
His teeth are like the stars,
They all come out at night.

December 15

LONG IN THE TOOTH

As with most of God's creatures,
Our gums recede when we ages,
Hence the unfortunate phrase,
"Long in the tooth,"
describing life's latter stages.

December 16

HABLA ESPANOL?

The Latino population
of the United States
Is steadily on the rise,
So founding of the
Hispanic Dental Association
Should come as no surprise.

December 17

RECENT FORMATION

Established in 1990,
HDA members are intent on serving
This country's 40 million Latin Americans
To whom their devotion is passionately unswerving.

December 18

DENTISTS OF COLOR

Even after the Civil War,
Black dentists were not admitted
To white dental societies anywhere in the Union
So founding *their own* professional entity
is that to which they committed.

December 19

FREE (TO JOIN) AT LAST!

In 1932, after many halting steps, a sustainable
Dental organization of African Americans—all free;
Was formally founded with help from
The Howard University College of Dentistry—in DC.

December 20

HERE TO STAY!

Today, the National Dental Association
and its auxiliaries—
Including dental assistants, hygienists, and students—
with justifiable pride,
Enjoys a membership of more than 7,000 professionals
Who serve a minority population
of more than 30 million—nationwide.

December 21

Family Dental Kits

In the late 19th and early 20th centuries
Mail order houses did a business quite brisk
Selling "...fillings for 20 teeth, instruments,
and full instructions on how to use—only $2.
Satisfaction guaranteed; no risk!"

December 22

WHAT IS A "PRECEPTOR"?

It's an expert, specialist, or teacher
Who gives practical training
to students or apprentices.
Before dental schools were established
in America—the world's first,
Non-formally trained preceptors provided
on-the-job instruction for new *dentistes*.

December 23

WHAT IS AN "EMPIRICIST"?

It's someone who practices dentistry or medicine
While disregarding scientific theory
And relies solely on practical experience.
They're also called "quacks" or "charlatans,"
and often resort to fraudery.

December 24

BEFORE *CONSUMER REPORTS*

So let's say that in 19th-century America
You're a preceptor-trained dental community member
And you observe all manner of empiricists
Bilking various and sundry citizens
of their hard-earned legal tender.

December 25

E PLURIBUS UNUM!

To protect the public, shut down the empiricists,
And safeguard the reputation of your chosen profession,
You and your colleagues do what comes naturally:
Establish a nationwide dental association.

December 26

COST-BENEFIT SHORTFALL

But back then a coast-to-coast trip
Meant two weeks of traveling—each way!
Never mind that it cost an arm and a leg;
Annual meeting attendance was
a tough decision to weigh.

December 27

THIRD TIME'S A CHARM

After a couple of false starts,
In 1859—on the eve of the war
which sundered the nation,
Twenty-six dentists convened in Niagara Falls
And founded the American Dental Association.

[N.B. The initial two (ultimately unsuccessful)
attempts at national dental organization were
the American Society of Dental Surgeons
and the American Dental Convention.]

December 28

GOING UP?

Picture the nail-pulling end of a crowbar

There's a dental instrument like that
(only smaller) called an "elevator," you see.

Used in lifting teeth for extraction—even today,

It was first described by Albucasis
(his Latin name) in the 10th Century AD.

December 29

FOUNTAINHEAD

While Dark-Age European
medical progress ground to a halt,

The Arab Muslim, Albucasis,

Produced a 30-volume illustrated opus,
The Method of Medicine.

In the parched intellectual desert
of the times, his work was like an oasis.

[N.B. Albucasis, born Abu al-Qasim Khalaf bin Abbas (936-1013 AD) and considered the greatest Muslim surgeon of all time, was born near Cordoba, Andalusia (now Spain). Physician to King Al-Hakam-II, another example of his contribution to dentistry included the invention of a set of 14 scalers.]

December 30

FISH STORY

When sharp tools became available
for removing tartar from teeth,

It was observed that the brittle, calcified residue

Literally popped off like the scales
of a fish being cleaned with a knife.

That's why today's dental professionals
refer to the process as "scaling."

[N.B. Although sharp stainless steel scalers are in general use today, diamond-tipped instruments were not uncommon two centuries ago when the temper of available metals was not high enough to hold an edge.]

December 31

TOP WORD

According to Merriam-Webster OnLine,

The word receiving more clicks on their website
than any other in 2005 was "integrity."

Year-after-year,
Gallup poll numbers consistently tell us,

That term *perfectly* characterizes
the profession of dentistry!

ACKNOWLEDGMENTS

I would like to take this opportunity to express my appreciation to the following individuals and organizations whose assistance has helped to make this book possible.

Rosemary Bray, consultant to the dental and orthodontic professions for her contribution of a "Painless Parker" quatrain.

Dr. James Brophy, Pierre Fauchard Academy, Editor, *Dental World,* for his private correspondence regarding the role of Pierre Fauchard in the history of dentistry.

Scherry G. Cooley, author, editor, and contributor to *Love Is the Best Medicine for Dental Patients and the Dental Team,* for her critique of an early manuscript of this book.

Alice Dible, wife of your author, constructive literary critic, graphics design consultant, mother, chef, nutritionist, auto fleet maintenance manager, business advisor, sounding board, interior decorator, gardening enthusiast, friend, and lover.

Sheri Doniger, DDS, Editor, *Woman Dentist Journal.*

Clifton O. Dummett, DDS, Distinguished Professor Emeritus, University of California School of Dentistry, for taking considerable time to evaluate this manuscript, for making several valuable recommendations on how it could be improved, for supplying me with reprints of more than a dozen professional journal articles dealing with the role of African Americans in the history of U.S. dentistry, and for providing a most welcome review of the finished work.

Richard A. Glenner, DDS, Past Historian, American Academy of the History of Dentistry, for his numerous recommendations on how this manuscript could be improved and for providing a most welcome review of the finished work.

Richard Golueke for his outstanding, creative illustrations and cover design.

Aletha Kowitz, retired former Director, Bureau of Library Services, American Dental Association, for her exceptional service as a volunteer proofreader and critique provider.

The staff at the ADA Dept. of Library Services with special thanks to Mary Kreinbring, Director, and Andrea Matlak, Archivist, for their personal assistance with supporting documents.

Frances S. Lennie of Indexing Research for preparation of the excellent index for this book.

Calder Lowe, NPR prize-winning poet and Executive Editor of *The Montserrat Review* literary journal for her critique of an early manuscript of this book.

Frank O. Mason, Director, and John P. Glueckert, Assistant Dental Librarian, at the Jennifer Ann Wilson Dental Library and Learning Center at the University of Southern California.

The staff at the ADA Foundation with special thanks to R. Barkley Payne, Senior Director, and Dwight S. Edwards, Director of Development.

Malvin E. Ring, DDS, dental historian, for taking considerable time to evaluate this manuscript, for making several valuable recommendations on how it could be improved, and for providing a most welcome review of the finished work.

Ron Sims, Special Collections Librarian, Galter Health Sciences Library, Feinberg School of Medicine, Northwestern University, for his invaluable, last-minute input on G.V. Black.

The staff at the Louise M. Darling Biomedical Library serving the UCLA School of Dentistry.

Scott D. Swank, DDS, Curator, Julia L. Filz, Director of Communications, and the rest of the staff at The Dr. Samuel D. Harris National Museum of Dentistry.

Susan Urbanczyk, Director of Public Relations at the Academy of General Dentistry.

Bob Wroe, friend of more than thirty years, trivia aficionado, Samuel F.B. Morse authority, and proofreading nit-picker.

Finally, I would like to thank those who contributed to the successful completion of this work but whose names the bowels of my hard drive will not yield and which my exhausted "little gray cells" are unable to retrieve in time to make the printer's deadline. You all know who you are, and I apologize for not providing you with the recognition you richly deserve.

SELECTED BIBLIOGRAPHY

"abracadabra." *The Encyclopedia of Astrobiology, Astronomy and Spaceflight.* The Worlds of David Darling. 2005. <www.daviddarling.info/encyclopedia/A/abracadabra.html>

Academy of General Dentistry. "A Millennium of Dentistry: A Look into the Past, Present and Future of Dentistry." 1996-2005. <www.agd.org/consumer/topics/history/millenium.asp>

Academy of General Dentistry. "How Can I Stop Grinding My Teeth at Night?" 1996-2005. <www.agd.org/consumer/topics/bruxism/grinding.asp>

Academy of General Dentistry. "What Is Bruxism?" 1996-2005. <www.agd.org/consumer/topics/bruxism/main.asp>

"Acupuncture Facts." 2005. Los Angeles Chinese Learning Center. <http://chinese-school.netfirms.com/acupuncture-points.html>

Al-Ghazal, Sharif Kaf. "Al-Zahrawi (Albucasis): A Light in the Dark Middle Ages in Europe." University of Pittsburgh 2005. <www.pitt.edu/~super1/lecture/lec11241/>

American Academy of Periodontology. "Dental Implants: Teeth That Look and Feel Like Your Own." Chicago: AAP 2004. <www.perio.org/consumer/2m.htm>

American Association of Endodontists. "Endodontics: An Ancient Science." 2005. <www.aae.org/welcome/history.htm>

American Association of Endodontists. "Tooth Saving Tips." AAE Fact Sheet. Chicago: AAE 1997. <www.aae.org/NR/rdonlyres/2740A49D-F135-4C05-97EC-26B728B9E7CC/0/toothsavingtips.pdf>

American Dental Assistants Association. "Dental Assisting and the ADAA." 28 Dec. 2005. <www.dentalassistant.org/2005_history.html#ADAA%20History%20and%20Service>

American Dental Assistants Association. "Frequently Asked Questions." 28 Dec. 2005. <www.dentalassistant.org/2005_faq.html>

American Dental Association. "125th Anniversary Commemoration." *Journal of the American Dental Association* 108.4 (Apr. 1984): 473-586.

American Dental Association. "ADA Timeline." Chicago: ADA 1995-2005. <www.ada.org/ada/about/history/ada_timeline.asp>

American Dental Association. *History of Dentistry.* Chicago: ADA 1995-2005 <www.ada.org/public/resources/history/index.asp>

American Dental Association. "National Children's Dental Health Month." Chicago: ADA 1995-2005 <www.ada.org/prof/events/featured/ncdhm.asp>

American Dental Association. "Overview: Emblem/Insignia of Dentistry." Chicago: ADA 1995-2005. <www.ada.org/public/topics/emblem_dentistry.asp>

American Dental Hygienists' Association. "History of ADHA." 2005. <www.adha.org/aboutadha/history.htm>

Angier, Natalie. "Dentistry: Far Beyond Drilling and Filling." 2003. <www.geocities.com/drkhosla1/News/newsa164.html>

Asbell, Dr. Milton B. *Dentistry, A Historical Perspective: Being a Historical Account of the History of Dentistry from Ancient Times, with Emphasis upon the United States from the Colonial to the Present Period.* Bryn Mawr, PA: Dorrance & Company, Inc. 1988.

Baker, Peggy M. "The Ether War. "Pilgrim Society & Pilgrim Hall Museum. 2004-2005. <www.pilgrimhall.org/Ether1.htm>

Bean, James B. "The Aluminum Base." *Dental Cosmos.* 8.ns (1867): 470-3. <www.hti.umich.edu/cgi/t/text/pageviewer-idx?c=dencos&cc=dencos&idno=acf8385.0008.001&q1=bean&q2=aluminum&q3=artificial&frm=frameset&view=image&seq=489>

Bellis, Mary. "History of Dentistry and Dental Care." 2005. About, Inc. division of *The New York Times* <http://inventors.about.com/library/inventors/bldental.htm>

Besombes, Dr. André. *Pierre Fauchard: The First Dental Surgeon, His Work, His Actuality.* English translation: Phillipe de Gaillande and George Higué. Las Vegas, NV: Pierre Fauchard Academy. 1993.

Black, G.V. "The Effect of Oxidation on Cut Alloys for Dental Amalgams." *Dental Cosmos 38* (1896): 43-8. <www.hti.umich.edu/cgi/t/text/pageviewer-idx?c=dencos;cc=dencos;rgn=full%20text;idno=ACF8385.0038.001;didno=ACF8385.0038.001;view=image;seq=00000055>

Brånemark, Rickard, et al. "Osseointegration in Skeletal Reconstruction and Rehabilitation." *Journal of Rehabilitation Research and Development.* 38.2 March/April 2001. <www.vard.org/jour/01/38/2/brane382.htm >

Bremner, Maurice David Kaufman. *The Story of Dentistry: From the Dawn of Civilization to the Present.* Brooklyn, NY: Dental Items of Interest Publishing Co., Inc. 1939.

British Broadcasting Company. "Claudius Galen." 28 Dec. 2005. <www.bbc.co.uk/history/historic_figures/galen_claudius.shtml>

British Dental Association. "The Story of Dentistry: Dental History Timeline." London: BDA 2005. <www.bda.org/museum/>

Carlisle, Gene. *Why Doc Holliday Left Georgia.* Macon, GA: Carl Isle Publishing, Inc. 2004.

Carson, Gerald. *The Dentist and the Empress: The Adventures of Dr. Tom Evans in Gas-lit Paris.* Boston: Houghton Mifflin 1983.

"Chapin Aaron Harris." 2000-2005. Grieves Historical Collection, Health Sciences and Human Services Library, University of Maryland. <www.hshsl.umaryland.edu/resources/historical/grieves/collection.html>

Christen, Arden G. and Pronych, Peter M. *Painless Parker: A Dental Renegade's Fight to Make Advertising "Ethical."* Halifax, Nova Scotia: McCurdy Printing, Ltd. 1995.

City of Syracuse. "Syracuse Firsts [Hanchett Dental Chair-1840]." 2005. <www.syracuse.ny.us/syracuseFirsts.asp>

Cooke, William P., Piper, Henry H., Hadley, Amos I. "Obituary In Memory of Dr. G. V. Black." *Journal of the Allied Dental Societies* 10.4 (1915): 538. <www.lib.umich.edu/dentlib/denthist/articles/Cooke1915.html>

Currier, G. Fräns. "History and Dentistry." 47pp College of Dentistry, The University of Oklahoma 1984. <http://dentistry.ouhsc.edu/intranet-web/Courses/DSA8211/historyofdentistry.pdf>

de Vaux, Jean Claude. "A Remembrance." 2000. Pierre Fauchard Academy 2005. <www.fauchard.org/publications/remembrance.htm>

Delta Dental. "Common Dental Problems." 2005. <www.deltadentalins.com/health/common_problems.html>

Delta Dental Plan of New Jersey. "A True Gothic Tale." 2005. <http://deltanj.com/kids_club/dental_trivia_copy20.shtml>

Delta Dental Plan of New Jersey. "Dental Trivia: Ancient Dentists." Nov. 2002. <www.deltadentalnj.com/kids_club/trivia_1102.shtml>

"Dental Cosmos." 2004. University of Michigan Dental Library. 2005. <www.hti.umich.edu/d/dencos/>

Dental ResourceNet. *The History of Dentistry.* Cincinnati, OH: Proctor & Gamble, Crest Learning Center. <www.dentalcare.com/ soap/lrncentr/timeline/TIMELINE5a.swf>

Dentist Guide Middle East. *The History of Dentistry*. Cairo, Egypt: Dentist Guide <http://dentistguideonline.com/ resaerches_articles/ dental_history/history_1.htm>

Dentistry Library, University of Michigan. "From Limericks to Lyricism: The Poetics of Dentistry and Oral Health." 28 Dec. 2005. <www.lib.umich.edu/dentlib/about/exhibits/poetry/>

Dentistry Library, University of Michigan. "Women in Dental History." 28 Dec. 2005. <www.lib.umich.edu/dentlib/about/ exhibits/dentfem/dentfemm.pdf>

Dougherty, Matthew. "A Biochemist Who Led Dental Education: William Gies' 1926 Report on Dental Education Is Still Relevant Today." *In Vivo,* Columbia University Health Sciences 2.6 (Mar. 2003). <www.cumc.columbia.edu/news/in-vivo/ Vol2_Iss06_mar26_03/medical-history.html#Anchor-11481>

Dunning, W.B. "Greene Vardiman Black." Journal of the Allied Dental Societies. 10.4 (Dec. 1915): 409-17. <www.lib.umich.edu/ dentlib/denthist/articles/Dunning1915.html>

Egyptian Museum. "HesiRe." Cairo, Egypt: IDSC 2001. <www.emuseum.gov.eg/details.asp?which2=585>

Evans, Thomas J. "Origin of the Word 'Anesthesia.' " 1998-2005. <www.anesthesia-nursing.com/anesth.html>

Evans, Thomas J. "The Unusual History of Ether." 1998-2005. <www.anesthesia-nursing.com/ether.html>

Fadl, Ayman. "Mummification in Egypt." Aldokkan. 2001-2005. <www.aldokkan.com/religion/mummy.htm>

Foley, Gardner P.H. *Foley's Footnotes: A Treasury of Dentistry.* Wallingford, PA: Washington Square East, Publishers, 1972.

Geissler, Paul. "A Glasgow Dentist an Edinburgh Legacy." Oct. 2001. History of Dentistry Research Group, University of Glasgow, Scotland 2005. <www.rcpsglasg.ac.uk/hdrg/2001Oct2.htm>

Glenner, Richard A., Davis, Audrey B., Burns, Stanley B. *The American Dentist: A Pictorial History with a Presentation of Early Dental Photography in America.* Missoula, MT: Pictorial Histories Publishing Co. 1990.

Glenner, Richard A. "How It Evolved: Connections [in] Dentistry and Medicine." *Journal of the History of Dentistry* 49.2 (Jul. 2001): 75.

Glover, Barbara, "George Washington—A Dental Victim." *The Riversdale Letter* Summer/Fall 1998. <www.americanrevolution.org/dental.html>

Goldstein, Joseph L. "How a Jolt and a Bolt in a Dentist's Chair Revolutionized Cataract Surgery." *Nature Medicine* 10.10 (Oct. 2004): xix-xx. <www.laskerfoundation.org/awards/naturemedicine/Goldstein.pdf>

Handelman, Stanley L. and Shey, Zia. "Michael Buonocore and the Eastman Dental Center: A Historic Perspective on Sealants." *Journal of Dental Research* 75.1 (1996): 529-34. <http://jdr.iadrjournals.org/cgi/reprint/75/1/529?maxtoshow=&HITS=10&hits=10&RESULTFORMAT=&author1=handelman&fulltext=buonocore+eastman&searchid=1136189517221_66&FIRSTINDEX=0&sortspec=relevance&volume=75&firstpage=529&journalcode=jdent>

Henderson, D. "Greene Vardiman Black (1836-1915), The Grand Old Man of Dentistry." PubMedCentral *Medical History* 5.2 (1961): Apr. 132-143. <www.pubmedcentral.nih.gov/articlerender.fcgi?artid=1034601>

Hendricks, Robert. *The Facts on File Encyclopedia of Word and Phrase Origins.* 3rd ed. New York: Checkmark Books, Facts on File, Inc. 2004.

Heynick, Frank. "Doc Holliday—150 Years Old." Pierre Fauchard Academy, 2001. <www.fauchard.org/publications/doc_holliday.htm>

Hillson, Simon. *Dental Anthropology.* New York: Cambridge University Press, 1996.

Hispanic Dental Association. "About HAD." 28 Dec. 2005. <www.hdassoc.org/site/epage/8345_351.htm>

Holladay, April. "Rabbit Teeth." *Wonder Quest with April Holladay.* 24 Jan. 2001. <www.wonderquest.com/RabbitTeeth.htm>

"Horace Hayden." 2000-2005. Grieves Historical Collection, Health Sciences and Human Services Library, University of Maryland. 2005. <www.hshsl.umaryland.edu/resources/historical/grieves/collection.html>

Hubar, J.S. "C. Edmund Kells, Jr., Pioneer in the Field of Dental X-rays." *Journal of the History of Dentistry* 48.1 (Mar. 2000): 11-15.

Hubble, Sue. "Let Us Now Praise the Romantic, Artful, Versatile Toothpick." *Smithsonian Magazine.* Jan. 1997.

Hyson, John M. and Davis, Audrey B. "Basil Manly Wilkerson: Dental Inventor Extraordinaire." *Journal of the History of Dentistry* 47.2 (Jul. 1999): 61-64. <http://dentistguideonline.com/resaerches_articles/ dental_history/history_1.htm> [sic]

Hyson, John M., Jr. and Whitehorne, Joseph W.A. "The 'Amex' Cast Aluminum Denture of World War I." *Journal of the History of Dentistry* 49.2 (Jul. 2001): 89-90.

Hyson, John M., Jr. "Man and Pain: Eternal Partners." *Journal of the History of Dentistry* 49.3 (Nov. 2001): 115-21.

International Medical and Dental Hypnotherapy Association. "Mission Statement." 2005. <www.imdha.com/mission.htm>

Johns Hopkins Medicine. "The Four Founding Physicians." 2005. <www.hopkinsmedicine.org/about/history/history5.html>

Jones, Terry. "Apollonia." The Catholic Community Forum. 2005. <www.catholic-forum.com/saints/sainta13.htm>

Kelleher, Tom. "Dentistry in Early 19th Century New England." 1998. Old Sturbridge Village 2005. <http://outdoorhistory.org/learning/DocumentViewer.php?Action=View&DocID=2011>

Kirsch, J.P. "St. Apollonia." *The Catholic Encyclopedia Vol. I.* New York: Robert Appleton Company. 1907. Online Edition, K. Knight 2003. <www.newadvent.org/cathen/01617c.htm>

Kuster, Curtis G. and Harn, Stanton D. "The Mention of Teeth in the Bible." *Bulletin of the History of Dentistry.* 39:1 (Apr. 1991): 17-9.

Larsen, Clark Spencer, et al. *Bioarchaeology: Interpreting Behavior from the Human Skeleton.* New York: Cambridge University Press, 1997.

Legends of America. "Doc Holliday—Deadly Doctor of the Old West." 2005. <www.legendsofamerica.com/CP-DocHolliday.html>

Leinfelder, Karl. "Alternatives to Crown and Bridge." Online posting. 23 Oct. 2005. <www.dentalblogs.com/archives/karl/alternatives-to-crwon-and-bridge/> [sic]

Lemire, Paula Anne Sharkey. "The White Martyrdom of Kateri Tekakwitha." Catholic Online 23 May 2004. <www.catholic.org/featured/headline.php?ID=980>

Lienhard, John H. "Dentistry." Engines of Our Ingenuity, University of Houston. 1988-1999. <www.uh.edu/engines/epi1455.htm>

Lister, Joseph *Antiseptic Principle of the Practice of Surgery.* London: 1867. *Internet Modern History Sourcebook,* Paul Halsall, Compiler, Fordham University, 1998. <www.fordham.edu/halsall/mod/1867lister.html>

"Listerine: History" 2005. Pfizer Australia, Inc. 2005. <www.pfizer.com.au/Products/Listerine/History.aspx>

Loh, Jules. "Reverend Spooner's Tips of the Slung" *Reader's Digest.* Feb. 1995. History of Spoonerisms. <www.fun-with-words.com/spoon_history.html>

London, Jack. *The Cruise of the Snark: Jack London's South Sea Adventure.* Mechanicsburg, PA: Stackpole Books. Reprint, 2001.

Macrone, Michael. Brush Up Your Bible. New York: Gramercy. 1998. <www.gracecathedral.org/enrichment/brush_excerpts/brush_ 20050621.shtml>

Marr, John. "Dentures of Death: A Historical Tragedy." *SF Life* 28 Feb. 2001 <www.sfbg.com/SFLife/35/22/lead.html>

Maryville University, Saint Louis. "Maryville Concurrent History (Silas Noble and J. P. Cooley patent toothpick manufacturing machine in 1872)." 2005. <www.maryville.edu/alumni/sbcontent/connections/history/concurrent.htm>

Medical Museum University of Iowa. "College of Dentistry: Early Equipment." 2005. <www.uihealthcare.com/depts/medmuseum/galleryexhibits/centuryofcaring/collegeofdentistry/02objects.html>

McCoy, John. "The Ether Monument, Boston Public Gardens." 1997. <www.mccoy.pair.com/personal/ether.html>

Moore, E. Drew. "History of Tooth Replacement and Dental Implants and Current Status of Dental Implants." Ft. Leavenworth, KS: U.S. Army Command and General Staff College. 2003 16pp. <http://medicalservicecorps.amedd.army.mil/leader_development/cgsc_research_papers/moore-history_of_tooth_replacement.doc>

M'Quillen, J.H. "Hullihen's Scriptural Explanation of the Cause of Dental Caries." *Dental Cosmos* 3 (1862): 153-4.

Moriyama, N. and Hasegawa, M. "The History of the Characteristic Japanese Wooden Denture." *Bulletin of the History of Dentistry* 35.1 (Apr. 1987): 9-16.

National Dental Association. "History." 28 Dec. 2005. <www.ndaonline.org/history.asp>

Neithercut, W. "Dental Themes on Stamps." Apr. 2000. History of Dentistry Research Group, University of Glasgow, Scotland 2005. <www.rcpsglasg.ac.uk/hdrg/April4.htm>

[N.B. This is probably the only time in your life that you'll find a note in the middle of a bibliography. I wonder how many readers will actually see this! In the context of the preceding citation, a person from Glasgow is called a *Glaswegian*.]

Olson, Daniel. "The History of Hypnosis." 28 Dec. 2005 <www.danielolson.com/hypnosis/hypnosis_history.html>

Pader, M. "Dentifrices." *Kirk-Othmer Encyclopedia of Chemical Technology,* 4th Ed. Vol. 7. New York: John Wiley & Sons, Inc. 1994. 1023-30

Paladin, Pam. "Orthodontic History: Braced for a Century, Orthodontists Mark Centennial of Dentistry's Oldest, Largest Specialty." AAO. 2005. <www.braces.org/history/>

Paul, Lee. "John Henry Holliday: The Living Dead Man." 2005. <www.theoutlaws.com/outlaws5.htm>

Penglase, Joanna. "The Poor Girls & Their Teeth! A Visit to the Dentist." The Jane Austen Society of Australia Inc. (JASA) 1 Aug. 2004 <www.jasa.net.au/london/dentist.htm>.

Phaneuf, Melissa. "Waubeka Officials Expecting 10,000 Flag Day Celebrants." JSOnline, Milwaukee: *Journal Sentinel* 3 Jun. 2002. <www.co.ozaukee.wi.us/history/FlagDay.htm>

Prinz, Hermann. *Dental Chronology: Record of the More Important Historic Events in the Evolution of Dentistry*. Philadelphia: Lea & Febiger, 1945.

"Protecting Children's Teeth Amid the Post-Halloween Candy Frenzy." San Diego: Children's Hospital and Health Center. 1 Oct. 2000. <www.chsd.org/1569.cfm>

Puki Ariki. "A Career to Get Your Teeth into—Betty Hammonds, Dental Nurse." 2005. <www.pukeariki.com/en/resources/treasurelink/tl070605.asp>

Raper, HR. "Practical Clinical Preventive Dentistry Based upon Periodic Roentgen-ray Examinations." *Journal of the American Dental Association*. (Sep. 1925): 1084-1100.

Renfrew, Jane, et al. *Food and Cooking in 16th-Century Britain: History and Recipes*. London: English Heritage Publications, 1985. <www.vanishedwood.org/guild/sugar.htm>

Ring, Malvin E. *Dentistry: An Illustrated History*. New York: Harry N. Abrams, Inc. Reprint, 1992.

Ring, Malvin E. "Glimpses of Life in a Victorian Surgery." Apr. 2004. History of Dentistry Research Group, University of Glasgow, Scotland 2004. <www.rcpsglasg.ac.uk/hdrg/2004April5.htm>

Ring, Malvin E. and Hurley, N. "James Beall Morrison: The Visionary Who Revolutionized the Practice of Dentistry." *JADA The Journal of the American Dental Association* 131.8 (Aug. 2000): 1161-7.

Shands Health Care. "Dental Plaque Identification Procedure and Removal." 2003. <www.shands.org/health/information/article/003426.htm>

Silkroad Foundation. "Porcelain and Its Spread to the West." 1997-2000. <www.silkroadfoundation.org/toc/index.html>

Simons, Martha Ann. "Cradle of the Rubber Industry." The Naugatuck Historical Society. 2005. <http://naugatuckhistory.com/hi-cradle_of_the_rubber_industry.htm>

Skinner, Richard Cortland. *A treatise on the human teeth, concisely explaining their structure and cause of disease and decay to which is added the most beneficial and effectual method of treating all disorders incidental to the teeth and gums; with directions for their judicious extraction and proper mode of preservation: interspersed with observations interesting to, and worthy the attention of, every individual.* New York: Johnson & Stryker for the author. 1801.

Slack, Charles. *Noble Obsession: Charles Goodyear, Thomas Hancock, and the Race to Unlock the Greatest Industrial Secret of the Nineteenth Century.* New York: Hyperion, 2002.

Straight Dope Science Advisory Board. "What's the Origin of the Tooth Fairy?" *The Straight Dope.* 20 Jul. 2004. <www.straightdope.com/mailbag/mtoothfairy.html>

Syn, Meng and Gray, Regina. "Weird Dental Facts." 1998. <www.carabelli.com/dental/dtrivia.htm>

Szaferek, Bernice. "Sealants." 2005. <www.szafarekdental.com/newsletters/col_news20030602.html>

The Art Institute of Chicago. "Art Access: Grant Wood, American, 1891-1942." 2004. <www.artic.edu/artaccess/AA_Modern/pages/MOD_5.shtml#>

The Dr. Samuel D. Harris National Museum of Dentistry. "The National Museum of Dentistry." 2005. University of Maryland. <www.dentalmuseum.umaryland.edu/>

"The Edwin and Trudy Weaver Historical Dental Museum." 2005. Temple University School of Dentistry. <www.temple.edu/dentistry/museum.htm>

The National Flag Day Foundation. "Bernard J. Cigrand." 2005. <www.nationalflagday.com/bjc.asp>

The Nobel Foundation. "History of the Nobel Foundation." 2005. <http://nobelprize.org/nobel/nobel-foundation/history/index.html>

The Tech National Museum of Innovation. "Charles D. Kelman, MD: Innovations in cataract surgical technology." 2005. <www.thetech.org/nmot/detail.cfm?ID=48&st=awardDate&qt=1991>

The University of Hong Kong Libraries. "Dental Library: e-Exhibition on Dental Library Rare Books." 2005. <http://lib.hku.hk/denlib/exhibition/rarebook/gen1.html>

"Toothbrush History." 1999-2005. BrushBrushBrush, Inc. <www.toothbrushexpress.com/html/toothbrush_history.htm>

Twain, Mark. "Some Rambling Notes of an Idle Excursion." *Atlantic Monthly*, Oct. 1877-Jan. 1878.

Udovitch, Mim. "Rosie O'Donnell." *Us Magazine* Oct.1997 <www.acmewebpages.com/rosie/9710__us.htm>

University of Bridgeport. "History of the Fones School of Dental Hygiene." 28 Dec. 2005. <www.bridgeport.edu/pages/2309.asp>

University of Iowa Hospitals and Clinics. "College of Dentistry: Early Equipment—Dental Foot Engine." 2002. <www.uihealthcare.com/depts/medmuseum/galleryexhibits/centuryofcaring/collegeofdentistry/02objects.html>

University of Minnesota, School of Dentistry, Oral Health Clinical Research Center. "Causes of Bad Breath (Halitosis)." 28 Dec. 2005 <www.dentistry.umn.edu/news_and_events/wcco_story_bad_breath.html>

University of Minnesota, School of Dentistry, Oral Health Clinical Research Center. "Treatment of Bad Breath." 28 Dec. 2005 <www.dentistry.umn.edu/news_and_events/wcco_story_bad_breath>

"Vulcan." *Encyclopedia Mythica*. 2001. Encyclopedia Mythica Online. <www.pantheon.org/articles/v/vulcan.html>.

WebMD. "First aid for a tooth that has been completely knocked out." 2005. <www.webmd.com/hw/health_guide_atoz/sig240330.asp>

Wells, Rosemary. "The Tooth Fairy Museum: An Historically Important Collection." *Bulletin of the History of Dentistry* 43.1 (Mar. 1995): 36-9.

"William Thomas Green Morton." *Appleton's Cyclopedia of American Biography*. 1887-1889. Virtualology.com. Envisum Inc. 2000. 28 Dec. 2005 <www.famousamericans.net/williamthomasgreenmorton/>

Wilwerding, Terry. *The History of Dentistry 2001*. Omaha, NE: Creighton University School of Dentistry, 2001. <http://cudental.creighton.edu/htm/ history2001.pdf>

Wright D.W. "Early Dental Instruments." *Dental Historian*, 15 (Nov. 1988): 32-49

Wynbrandt, James. *The Excruciating History of Dentistry: Toothsome Tales & Oral Oddities from Babylon to Braces*. New York: St. Martin's Griffin, 1998.

INDEX

abrasives, 112
Academy of General Dentistry (AGD), 136
Academy of Osseointegration, 136
acupuncture, 5
Adams, John, 94
adults, number of teeth in, 110
Aesculapius, 39
African Americans, 101-102, 178
air abrasion, 52
Albucasis, 182
alcohol, 79, 169
aluminum dentures, 21
amalgam fillings, 30-31
American Academy of Periodontology, 142
American Association of Orthodontists (AAO), 74
American Dental Assistants Association (ADAA), 118
American Dental Association (ADA), 117, 136, 156, 181
American Dental Protective Society, 150
"Amex" dentures, 21
ammonia, 10
anesthesia:
    alcohol providing, 79, 169
    nitrous oxide, 58
    origin of word, 59
Angle, Edward Hartley, 71-75
animal teeth, 98, 167
    as dentures, 125
antimicrobials, 10
antiseptics, 13, 14, 15
Apollonia of Alexandria, 22-23
aqua fortis, 12
Aristotle, 110
Arnold, Esther Watkins, 4
Arthur, Robert, 100
"The Athlete" (Rodin sculpture), 103
Atlanta Midwinter Clinic, 153
Aylmer (Bishop of London), 55

baby teeth. *see* first teeth
Bacon, Josiah, 150-151
    murder of, 151-152
bacteria, 40, 96, 140-141
bad breath. *see* halitosis
Baker, Bill, 166-167
Baltimore College of Dental Surgery, 96, 100
barber-surgeons, 12
Bean, Dr. James Baxter, 20
The Bible, 22, 126
bicuspids, 69
bite pressure, 51
bitewings, 38
Black, Dr. Greene Vardiman, 26-30
Black, Dr. Thomas, 27
Blanc, Mel, 167
Boke of Nurture (Rhodes), 36
Bonaparte, Louis-Napoleon, 172-173
bone grafts, 142
bow drill, 33
Braid, James, 131
Brånemark, Per-Ingvar, 134-136
bridgework, 35, 42, 44, 77
brushing teeth:
    ancient Greeks and, 113
    ancient Romans and, 107
    campaign to ensure, 108
    checking results, 47
    incentive for child, 52
    as preventive measure, 51
bruxism, 158, 160
    joke about, 159

Bryant, William Cullen, 36
buccal surface, 69
buck teeth, 75
Bugs Bunny, 167
Buonocore, Michael, 31

C. Edmund Kells Honor Society. *see* Kells, C. Edmund, Jr.
calcium carbonate, 140
calculus, 68
candy, and caries, 133, 153
canines. *see* conical teeth
car racing, 95
carbolic acid (phenol), 13
caries:
- candy and, 133, 153
- oral hygiene and, 121
- removing, 32, 33, 96
- sugar and, 55

Carson, Gerald, 174
cataract surgery, 161-162
caustic agents, 164
cautery, 127
cavities:
- caries removal from, 32, 96
- cauterization of, 127
- Chinese epidemic, 133

Celsus, Cornelius, 79
Chalfant, Dr. Samuel P., 151-152
"charlatans," 180-181
Chémant, Nicolas Dubois de, 129
"chew stick," 37
chewing, 56, 100
children:
- brushing teeth, 52
- dental prophylaxis for, 119-120
- National Children's Dental Health Month, 24
- number of teeth in, 110
- thumbsucking by, 75

China, 132, 133
Cigrand, Bernard J., 83
Cincinnati's Eclectic College of Medicine (CECM), 144
Civil War:
- dental extractions in, 124
- dentition requirements for soldiers in, 98

cocaine, 60
Colgate Company, 105, 114
Colgate Dental Cream, 114
composite fillings, 30-31
conical teeth, 17, 69, 98
Connery, Sean, 37
Cooley, J.P., 170
cotton rolls, 155
Crest toothpaste, 105
Cummings, John A., 149
cuspids. *see* conical teeth

dandelions, 5
Dark Ages. *see* Middle Ages (500-1000 AD)
DDS (Doctor of Dental Surgery), 41, 96
Dean, James Byron, 77-78
deciduous teeth. *see* first teeth
'Demon offspring," 110
dent, 4
dent de lion (dandelion), 5
Dental Anatomy (Black), 30
dental appliances:
- mouthguard, 25
- nightguard, 160

dental assistants, 99, 116-118
dental chairs, 84-86, 103
Dental Cosmos (journal), 19, 20, 103
dental drills, 103
dental forensics, 44
dental hygiene. *see* oral hygiene
dental hygienists, 107, 119-120
- school for, 120-121

dental implants, 134-136
dental imprint, 97
dental kits, 179
dental offices, 142-143

dental plaque. *see* plaque
dental prosthetics, 54, 80. *see also* bridgework; dentures
dental records, 45
dental supplies, 109. *see also individually named equipment and supplies*
dental surgery, 85, 142
dentifrice, 112-113, 114. *see also* toothpaste
The Dentist and the Empress: The Adventures of Dr. Tom Evans in Gas-lit Paris (Carson), 174
dentist/dentistry, 4
    integrity of, 183
    official color of, 37
dentiste, 4
dentures:
    adjustment anecdote, 90-91
    aluminum, 20, 21
    "Amex," 21
    animal teeth as, 125
    iron, 22
    lost, 94
    vulcanite, 21, 148
    "Waterloo," 109
    for women, 67
    wooden, 46
diastema, 45
diethyl ether, 58
digestion, 56
disclosing tablets, 47
distal surface, 69
DMD *(Dentariae Medicinae Doctorae),* 41
DNA, 45
dogteeth. *see* conical teeth
Dogtoothed Violets, 5
Dr. Sheffield's Crème dentifrice, 114
drill(s):
    air abrasion, 52
    bow, 33
    finger, 32
    first electric, 36
    foot-treadle, 33, 47, 111
    sound effect, 52

Earp, Wyatt, 87
Eastman Dental Center, 31
electric drill, 36
elevator (instrument), 182
Elizabeth I, Queen of England, 55
empiricists, 180-181
enamel, 79
eruption of teeth, 110
Etruscan period, 54
Evans, Thomas Wiltberger, 171-174
excavation of teeth, 32, 33, 96
extraction of teeth:
    in ancient Greece, 39
    anesthetic for, 79
    in Civil War, 124
    early draft dodgers and, 98
    Elizabeth I of England and, 55
    instrumentation for, 123-124
    by Jack London, 66
    in 19th-century Italy, 44
    in Old West, 169
    by "Painless" Parker, 61
    as punishment, 22-23
eyeteeth. *see* conical teeth

facial muscles, 53
false teeth. *see* bridgework; dentures
family dental kits, 179
fangs. *see* conical teeth
Farrar, J.N., 71-75
Fauchard, Pierre (1678-1761), 6-10, 80, 89
filling(s), 79
    amalgam, 30-31
    composite, 31
    gold, 171
first teeth, 4, 49, 51, 110

Flagg, Josiah Foster, 85
Fletcher, Horace, 56
Florence Manufacturing Company, 64
flossing:
  ancient Romans and, 107
  campaign to ensure, 108
  checking results, 47
  incentive for child, 52
  as preventive measure, 45, 51
Foley, Gardner P.H., 125
Foley's Footnotes: A Treasury of Dentistry (Foley), 125
Fones, Alfred, 118-120
Fones School of Dental Hygiene, 121
food residue, 41
foot-treadle drill, 33, 47, 111
For All Kids Foundation, 16
Ford, Dr. Arthur C., 88
Formations of Poisons by Microörganisms (Black), 30
Fowler, Dr. Henry, 117
Franklin Institute, Philadelphia, 171
Freeman, Robert Tanner, 101-102
French Dental Guild, 8, 9

Galen, Claudius (c. 129-c. 216 AD), 17, 158
gambling, 87, 89
gaps in teeth, 45
gemstone onlays, 137
gender discrimination, 144
gingivitis, 140-141
gnashing of teeth. *see* bruxism
gold fillings, 171
Goodyear, Charles, 148-149
Goodyear Dental Vulcanite Company, 149-150, 152
Goodyear India Rubber Glove Company, 165
Goodyear Tire and Rubber Company, 148
Gray, Dr. Ida, 157
Gray, Pearl [Zane], 51
Greece, ancient, 39, 113
Green, George F., 36
Greenwood, Dr. John, 47, 96
gum grafts, 142
"gum scum." *see* plaque
gums, 140-141
  receding, 176

halitosis, 15, 16, 40, 41
Halloween candy, 153
Halstead, Dr. William S., 164-165
Hampton, Caroline, 164-165
Hanchett, Milton Waldo, 86
hand protection, 164
Harris, Chapin Aaron, 96, 113
Harris, Dr. Samuel D., 50
Hasegawa, M., 46
Hayden, Horace, 96
HesiRe, 3
Hippocrates, 126-127. *see also* toothpaste
Hispanic Dental Association (HDA), 177
Hobbes, Dr. Lucy Beaman, 144-146, 156
Holliday, Dr. Robert A., 89
Holliday, John Henry "Doc," 87-89
Holmes, Dr. Oliver Wendell, 59
Howard University College of Dentistry, 178
Hunter, John, 69
hypnodontics, 132
hypnotism, 130-131

ice hockey, 166-167
incisors, 69
indentured servants, 97
integrity, 183
inventions, 163
Iowa State Dental Society, 145
iron dentures, 22

Jackson, Charles T., 58
Jackson, C.T., 59
Jagger, Mick, 130
Jefferson, Thomas, 94
Jefferson Medical College, 171
Jeopardy! (TV show), 90
Jones, Emeline Roberts, 63
Jones & White, 19
Journal of the American Dental Association (JADA), 20

kaolin, 128
Kellogg, Dr. John Harvey, 56
Kells, C. Edmund, Jr., 99, 116
Kelman, Dr. Charles D., 161-163
kidney meridian, 5
Kingsley, Norman W., 71-75
Koeisha Ltd., Japan, 170

Lambert, Jordan Wheat, 15
Lambert Company, 15
The Lancet, 13
Larsson, Gösta, 136
latex, 148
laughing gas. *see* nitrous oxide
Lawrence, Dr. Joseph, 15
Le chirurgien dentiste (Fauchard), 6, 10, 80
Life of Bishop Aylmer (Strype), 55
lilac (color), 37
lingual surface, 69
"Lion's Tooth" (dandelion), 5
Lister, Joseph, 13, 14
Listerine, 15, 16
litigation, 150-151
London, Jack, 65-66
loose teeth, 141

Malocclusion of the Teeth (Angle), 74
marshmallow, 93
Martagne, General Comte de, 129
martyrs, 23
Maryland Bridge, 35
Mayans (c. 900 AD), 137
McAllister, Hall, 151-152
McKeeby, Dr. B. H., 84
McKey, Dr. John, 87
mesial surface, 69
The Method of Medicine (Albucasis), 182
mice, 51
microbes, 104, 108
Micro-Organisms of the Human Mouth (Miller), 108
microscope, 104
Middle Ages (500-1000 AD), 56, 110
milk teeth. *see* first teeth
Miller, Jack, 95
Miller, Willoughby Dayton, 108-109
molars, 69
Mona Lisa: The History of the World's Most Famous Painting (Sassoon), 175
Moriyama, N, 46
Morrison, James B., 33
Morse, Samuel S.F., 59
Morton, William Thomas Green, 58, 59
Moss, Alfred, 95
Moss, Sterling, 95
mouthguards, 25
mouthwash, 11, 93. *see also* Listerine
Mouton, Dr. Charles, 80
mummies, 42
murder, 151-152

Napoleon III, 172-174
National Association of Dental Faculties, 37
National Children's Dental Health Month, 24
National Flag Day, 82
National Museum of Dentistry exhibits, 50

Natural History of Teeth (Hunter), 69
Newman, Irene, 118-120
Newton, Sir Isaac, 50
nicotine stains, 161
nightguard, 160
nitric acid, 12
nitrous oxide, 57, 58
Nobel Prize winners, 38, 109
Noble, Silas, 170
Northwestern University, 26
Northwestern University Dental School, 26, 29
Novocain (procaine), 60

occlusal surface, 69, 160
occlusion, 73
O'Donnell, Rosie, 16
Ohio College of Dental Surgery (OCDS), 145, 146, 156
Ohio Journal of Dental Medicine, 116
Old West, tooth extraction in, 169
old wives tale, 80
onlays, 137
Opening of the Mouth ritual, 42
Operative Dentistry (Black), 30
oral cancer, 161
oral care products, 105, 108-109
oral hygiene:
  children and, 24, 119-120
  courtship and, 165
  gum disease and, 140-141
  in World War I, 104-105
  in World War II, 78
orthodontia, 70-71, 73
orthodontic problems, 70
Osengio, Brother Giovanni Battista, 44
osseointegration, 134-136

pain control:
  anesthetics for. *see* anesthesia
  hypnosis for, 130-131
painkillers, 59-60
paint tubes, 115
palate sensitivity, 60
Parker, Dr. Edgar R.R. ("Painless" Parker), 61
Pasteur, Louis, 13
patent infringement, 150-152
patron saint, 23
Peabody, --, 105, 113
Pelican "pliers," 123-124
periodontic treatment, 142
pets, teeth in, 98
phacoemulsification, 161-162
pharaohs, 3
Philip, Roman Emperor, 22-23
picking teeth, 36, 65
Pierre Fauchard Academy, 10
plaque, 30, 47, 64, 68, 104, 118, 140-141
Polo, Marco, 128
porcelain, 128-129
  teeth made from, 102, 129
Practical Guide to Operations on the Teeth (Snell), 85
preceptors, 180
pregnancy, 81
priests, 56
primary teeth. *see* first teeth
procaine (Novocain), 60
Procter & Gamble, 105
prostheses. *see* bridgework; dental prosthetics; dentures
proximal surface, 69
punishment, tooth extraction as, 22-23

"quacks," 180-181

rabbit teeth, 167
racial discrimination, 102, 178
Rand, John, 115
Raper, Dr. Howard Riley, 38
The Rationale of Nervous Sleep (Braid), 131
receding gums, 176

replantation of teeth, 6, 25
Revere, Paul, 43-44
Rhein, Dr. Meyer, 64
Rhodes, Hugh, 36
Riders of the Purple Sage (Gray), 51
Riggs, Dr., 58
Roizen, Dr. Michael F., 81
Rome (c. 200 AD), 22, 107
Röntgen, Wilhelm Conrad, 38
Ross, Elizabeth (Betsy) Griscom, 81
rubber gloves, 165
Russell, Dr. Stephanie, 81
Russell, Kurt, 166

St. Apollonia, 23
Sassoon, Prof. Donald, 175
sayings:
  "armed to the teeth," 96
  "bite the bullet," 98
  "chewing the fat," 42
  "long in the tooth," 176
  "skin of his teeth," 126
  "teeth on edge," 137
  "whiskey courage," 169
scalers, 182
scaling, 183
Schange, J.M. Alexis, 70
sealants, 38
Seegar, Dr. John A., 89
Seiberling, Frank, 148
Shakespeare, William, 137
Sheffield, Washington Wentworth, 114-115
"siwaks," 37
Skinner, Dr. Richard C., 54
smoking, 161
snaggletooth, 75
Snell, Dr. James, 85
soap, 105, 113
Southard, Juliette A., 117-118
Spears, Dr. J.C., 27
Spooner, Rev. William Archibald, 17
Spoonerisms, 17
S.S. White Dental Manufacturing Company, 19, 36, 102-103
stone-ground flour, 108
straightening teeth, 70
Strong Wood Products, 170
Strype, John, 55
succedaneous teeth, 110
sugar, 55
surfaces of teeth, 69
The Surgeon Dentist (Fauchard), 80

Taft, Dr. Jonathan, 156-157
Taixi point, 5
Talbot, Dr. Eugene Solomon, 38
Talmud, 41
tartar, 64, 68, 118, 140-141
  scalers for removal of, 182-183
Taylor, James M., 146
Taylor, Thomas B., 155
teeth cleaning. *see* brushing teeth; flossing; picking teeth; scaling
temporomandibular joint (TMJ), 74
Thomas P. Hinman Dental Meeting, 153
thumbsucking, 75
titanium dental implants, 134-135
tongue-scrapers, 37, 40
Tooth Fairy, 4, 5, 49
Tooth Fairy Museum, 5
tooth key, 124
tooth loss, 51, 80
Tooth Mouse (Mexico), 147
toothache:
  acupuncture point for, 5
  extraction and. *see* extraction of teeth
toothbrushes:
  early, 37
  materials for, 64, 132
toothpaste, 105
  historical forms, 112-113

toothpaste tubes, 115
toothpaste-in-a-jar, 114
toothpick museum, 170
toothpicks, 65, 170
Total toothpaste, 105
Treatise on the Human Teeth (Skinner), 54
Trebek, Alex, 90
trench mouth, 104
Twain, Mark, 137

University of Maryland Medical Center, 160
University of Michigan School of Dentistry, 157
urine, 10, 11, 112

volatile sulfur compounds (VSCs), 40
von Leeuwenhoek, Antonius, 104

Warren, Major General Joseph, 44
Washington, George, 46, 50
"Waterloo Denture," 109
Weaver, Dr. Robert C., 102
Weclew, Dr. Thaddeus V., 136
Wells, Dr. Rosemary, 5
Wells, Horace, 57, 58, 59
Wharton, Francis, 125
whiskey, 169
White, Samuel Stockton, 102, 171
White, Samuel Stockton, III, 103
Wilkerson, Professor Basil Manly, 86
Wilson, Woodrow, 82
Winter Olympiad (1980), 166
wisdom teeth, 69, 100
women:
  in dentistry, 116-119, 120, 144-146
  dentures and, 67
  number of teeth in, 110
  oral hygiene and motherhood, 80-81
Wood, Grant, 84
wooden dentures, 46
World War I, 21, 104-105
World War II, 78, 105

x-rays, 38, 99

ADA. | FOUNDATION

American Dental Association Foundation

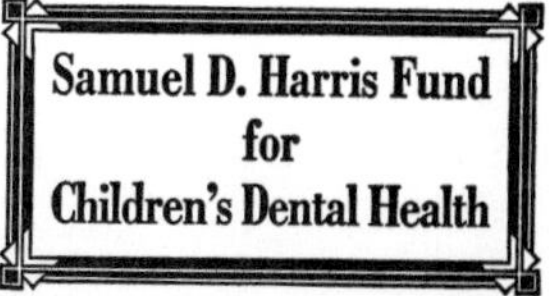

In the spirit of fostering more love in the world, a portion of the proceeds from sales of *The Dental Patient's Little Book of History, Humor and Trivia* will go to the Samuel D. Harris Fund for Children's Dental Health, a permanent endowment fund of the ADA Foundation. The primary objective of this program is the prevention of tooth decay and other oral diseases in children, particularly for those children whose economic status places them at greatest risk of not receiving adequate oral health education and access to preventive care.

The ADA Foundation is the charitable arm of the American Dental Association. As dentistry's premier philanthropic and charitable organization, the ADA Foundation champions health by securing contributions and providing grants for sustainable programs in dental research, education, access to care and assistance for dentists and their families in need. Its strategic ties with the American Dental Association strengthen the ADA Foundation's ability to improve health and make lives better.

The provision of grants for a wide range of philanthropic and charitable programs helps to improve oral disease knowledge and increases both access to, and the quality of, dental care for all populations. By fostering continuous advancement in dental research, education, access to care, and charitable assistance, the Foundation significantly contributes to improved oral health and the practice of dentistry.

ADA Foundation
Samuel D. Harris Fund for Children's Dental Health
211 E. Chicago Avenue
Chicago, IL 60611
Phone: 312.440.2547 • Fax: 312.440.3526
Email: adaf@ada.org